THE
LIGHT
OF
NAVIGATION

Spiritual Direction in Tough Times

MARGUERITE LEVER-WOODALL

ISBN 978-1-63903-314-0 (paperback)
ISBN 978-1-63903-315-7 (digital)

Christian Faith Publishing
832 Park Avenue
Meadville, PA 16335
www.christianfaithpublishing.com

Printed in the United States of America

CONTENTS

Acknowledgments 7
Preface..9

The Vision of the Storm...13
God and the Lighthouse...15
An Open Letter..18
The Control Factor Illusion..20
God and the GoFundMe...23
The Eye of the Storm 26
God and the Funeral Song..29
He Grieves with Me 32
Where the Good Things Are 37
God and Capital One..42
The Two Paths of Brokenness..45
When God Goes Before You 48
God, the Banquet, and the Frogman 53
Requiem for a Future 59
The Oaks of Righteousness 62
Jesus and the Justice Economy..69
The Last Thanksgiving..72
The Holiday Voice 75
Is There Room at the Inn?..77
God and the Arms of Communion 78
The Wailing Bench...80
Dear Reader 84
Many Worlds, One Kingdom..88
God and the Favorite Photo 90
Sorrow's Altar 95

The D-Word 97
Never Meant to Be 98
God and the Two-Step Victory...99
Choose Life..102
God and the Time Clock Redemption 105
The Travelers..111
Another Country...112
God, Delta Air Lines, and Both Escorts...............................114
The Three Images of Grief 117
The Sanballat Factor..119
God and the Liar...124
Run the Race..131
God, the Three Witnesses, and…......................................133
The Message for Me 137
The Gentle Breeze...139
The Scroll of Destiny 143
The Valued...144
Safely Home..147
The Message...151

ACKNOWLEDGMENTS

To those I've loved and lost. How I miss you.
Mom, Dad, Randy (my soul mate), and my son Randall. Thank
you for being a part of my life journey here. I know I will
see you again, and I also know you are watching. Hopefully,
I will run this race to its conclusion and finish it well.

Dearest Mary, I will forever remember your love and
strength to look upon for me what I could not.

Kenton Lor, your generous offer to proof read for me was
immeasurably helpful, and I learned a great deal from
it. You and your precious wife, my dear friend Choua,
have blessed me, and I will forever love your people.

PREFACE

As I woke briefly during the night, I sensed a presence in my room. God was speaking to me in a dream as He sometimes does. During the dream, I saw myself standing with a crowd of African American people surrounding a black woman who was sitting down among them on the ground. She had in her lap a neatly folded, gray pullover-hooded sweatshirt. The front, the sweatshirt had a photo imprinted on it, and it was of her deceased son. I walked up and gently took the shirt from her lap and clutched it tightly over my chest and sobbed openly and loudly as I held it.

The deepest grief for this woman's loss had gripped my soul. At the same time, the grief racked my body physically as I slept in my bed. After a time, I handed it carefully back into her possession and said, "I am so very sorry for your loss." Everyone standing around me was taken aback by the genuine grief I had shown for this woman's family. The loss of my own son to a drug overdose had opened my heart to others' sorrow and pain.

I have had an "average" human compassion for others but not a deeply felt one. Much can be gained in the midst of tragedy. One of them is compassion for others and their suffering. Our own suffering changes everything. The compassion of Christ growing in us through it supersedes all racial, religious, political, and personal boundaries of mistrust. It was one famous preacher who said that "God can turn our scars into stars." He's right.

Tragedy can break you, and you never fully recover, or it can make you. God spoke to me one day when I was praying about a bully at my son's school who was causing harm. I did not want Randall to go through what I did with bullying as a child and young adult in school. I'll never forget what He said: "Marguerite, adversity can breed champions."

This book is a collection of memories about a life's journey, which includes the thoughts, emotions, and experiences involved in the grief when we lose someone we love deeply. It is certainly not the sum total of all of them, but it is what I have felt led by the Lord to share with others in the current times we live in. I have tried in these writings or short stories to give a voice to what some of us experience in life when hardship or tragedies occur. You know, the inner thoughts we all have in these events that we don't feel we can share easily. Somehow, it is easier to walk through hard and difficult times when someone else gives a voice to what we are truly feeling on the inside. My hope is that others will know they are not alone in their pain, and there is a God who truly loves us and is walking with us through our deepest, darkest moments. So few people even recognize that God's movements touch us daily.

Which leads me to the second reason I wanted to write this book and the most important one. If we allow Him to help us navigate through this life with all of its problems, accidents, and tragedies, then we are winners of the best kind. Christ is truly the best "light of navigation" in this fallen world.

This is also a collection of those small insights that God gives in our daily walk with Him if we let Him speak to us in a deeply personal way. Few would give God the time of day, much less develop a friendship with Him. It is my hope that others will see God "in the midst" of every circumstance in their lives. His attention to detail is astounding and His love amazing. I've tried to convey in the following stories how God has intervened in my life many times through the tragedies themselves. His loving-kindnesses are very great.

Loving-kindness in its interpretation in the Scriptures can be understood in the picture of someone being lovingly useful or meeting a need, large or small, when it is needed the most. He walks with us so much more than we know and perceive. I've been privileged to experience it and more importantly, see it. In the Greek language, it is called the *perichoresis* or the dance. At traditional Greek weddings, the *perichoresis* is traditionally performed. It is a dance that starts in circles, weaving in and out in a very beautiful pattern of motion. The dance goes faster and faster, all the while staying in perfect rhythm and in sync with each other.

There is a divine "rotation" or going around in a dance with God in our lives. He weaves in and out and through our daily living. Ironically, when my son passed, it was in that tragedy that I began to see and know firsthand how much God truly loves me. As Christians, we are taught that He loves us but experientially; I did not know the depth of the love of God until then. I had never known such a love before this. A by-product of these experiences has been a thankful heart attitude toward God, which I have found will usher me into His presence quickly and continuously in my daily life.

This book is also about the *perichoresis*. Have you seen it? Have you felt it? Has it put its arms around you and you did not recognize it? I pray God will open your eyes to His divine movements on your behalf, not only in the future but in the past where those moments may have been missed altogether. Perhaps what you thought was coincidence was actually *the dance*.

THE VISION OF THE STORM

It was October 2, 2016, and the drive to church on this particular morning was different. As I drove on the highway, a panoramic scene or vision began to play out in front of me. At the same time, a narrative began from the Lord as I looked at what He was revealing.

I saw a majestic tall red-and-white-striped lighthouse, its light beaming brightly. It sat anchored on a large rock formation just off-shore from a main shoreline or beach. There was a fierce storm, and waves were breaking against the lighthouse, and it was getting very dark. I heard the Lord speaking about "the Light of Navigation," that Christ is the only true light of navigation in this life we live.

I also saw giant bonfires blazing on a beach in a harbor far-ther down from the lighthouse and its location. The bonfires blazed brightly as a storm was moving in. Pirates or local natives would light these fires with the intent to deceive and lure any nearby ship, trying to escape an incoming storm, into sailing into their harbor instead of the lighthouse's.

The bonfires were mimicking the lighthouse's illumination and the harbor it pointed to. These pirates or natives knew that there were dangerous reefs underwater in their harbor that would rip apart incoming ships that were trying to avoid the storm's fierceness. By using the bonfires as a reference for navigation to another possible safe haven rather than the lighthouse, unsuspecting ships would sail into the waters with these unseen massive underwater reefs and would be torn apart.

After the ship was wrecked, all the pirates or natives had to do was wait for the ship's contents to wash ashore to take their plunder. The historical information about the pirates and natives was some-thing I did not know about until the Lord shared it with me in the vision. The message was clear. We are not to be deceived by the false lights that the spiritual enemy of our souls tries to guide us with.

We all experience shipwrecks in life; they happen for many reasons. Some occur because we thought we had the Lord's direction and later realized it was not Him guiding us. While other shipwrecks occur when life's tragedies strike suddenly, and we can be at a loss as to what direction to go in afterward in our journey. I asked the Lord, "How do we know when the enemy is putting out a false light of navigation with his lies and deceptions?"

He said, "Most often, it is the quick, easy, or convenient path that is illuminated. And few see My light of navigation in the midst of the storm because they're too busy trying to avoid the storm altogether. Christ is your light of navigation!"

I knew it was important to share this vision with my fellow church members in the service that day, and I was allowed to speak to the congregation to share it with them just before our time of worship began.

My son Randall died today. It happened during the minutes that I shared the message of this vision. This message from the Lord was also for me.

GOD AND THE LIGHTHOUSE

Focus or lack thereof—this has been an issue in my life that I've battled frequently. Many times, I've verbally confessed to being easily distracted, or something captures my attention way too quickly. I wish I hadn't. That confession can invite the enemy of our souls to oblige us with lots of distractions or diversions. In my time of devotions in the morning, I struggle with competing thoughts about anything else going on but praying and communing with God. A thought pops up, and I'm following it until I rein it in and refocus again on my task at hand. I smile or laugh when someone uses the expression and shouts out, "Squirrel!" when they're observing someone going down a rabbit hole in their thought processes and forget what they're doing.

It's a serious issue, though, especially when walking the path as a Christian. There is so much around us in this world vying for our full attention. We are, as a whole, so very easily distracted by everything going on around us at any given moment. There's easily accessible entertainment at our fingertips that has captured the world's mind; just flick a switch or push a button. For some time, I've guarded my mind with how much I'm watching television on any given day.

Then there are the storms of life that this world brings that make us feel like we're being blown way off course. All we can see or focus on is the storm itself and its darkness. No one goes through this life journey without a storm. Some of us go through many of them over a period of time, others only a few.

I'm reminded of Job, who went through a rapid series of life storms, one right after another, and in a single day lost everything he had. This included ten children, eleven thousand various livestock, and many servants. To add insult to his injury, a short time later, he was afflicted with boils from the top of his head to the soles of his feet. All he could do was sit in an ash heap, scraping the boils with a potsherd while visiting friends tried to offer advice and possible reasons why he was going through such adversity. Only one friend among them did not put the blame on Job for his misfortunes.

Even as I write this, the memory of another dream returns that I had years ago, and it occurred more than once, and I instinctively knew it was from God. In the dream, I was driving on an elevated stretch of highway with a large valley below and to my right. As I looked out of the passenger window at the vast scene of this beautiful valley area, I saw square plots of farmland where farmers had plowed or planted different crops. Dirt roads crisscrossed the acres, and occasional farm homes were scattered throughout as well as towns visually in the distance. It was the quintessential checkerboarded country landscape.

The scene before me then changed, and I saw massive amounts of tornadoes touching down on the valley's landscape. There were literally tornadoes touching down in the center of every square mile of land. The beautiful valley was full of them, and one could not drive through it without encountering one. The scene overall also took on an ominous darkness. I believe that perhaps I was seeing the future (which may be upon us now) as Christ's return becomes more imminent, and at the same time viewing my own path in the future where God's guidance would be much needed.

There are storms everywhere in most people's lives, and they are increasing. We can see them worldwide as well. They can bring unprecedented destruction on a personal and community level. The time is now at hand when the only way to get through the multiplicity of these fierce storms is to keep our focus on Christ.

On the day of my son's funeral, at the hospice pastor's insistence, I found myself led to a side room in the funeral home. He had emphasized the importance of praying with us before the service started that day. I hadn't been in this room before with its finely appointed furnishings. The funeral home was much larger than most others I've seen over the years and was very spacious. There were many rooms for visitations and meetings. I hadn't even begun to see them all, and I didn't need to.

Most of the time, I kept to the entryway, the main office, and the chapel itself. The hospice pastor seemed like a kind and gentle man; however, I had not spent much time with him because of pressing preparations. He knew nothing about me, and any comments he made during the service I had asked to be directed toward the salvation of others in attendance if possible. I did learn, however, that he knew some close Christian friends of mine in the area. Small world.

As the pastor faced me with my sister by my side, several of my son's friends who were chosen as pallbearers gathered with us as well. Before beginning any prayer, he stepped toward me with a strength of purpose, looked at me intently, and spoke with what I recognized immediately as a word from God. The deliberate and power-filled statement he made stunned me; it took me aback, and he declared with authority, "Marguerite, know this: that in the midst of this storm in your life, always remember that Christ is your lighthouse!"

As he spoke, he lifted his arm, and with his hand, pointed across the room to an end table by a large sofa. I turned and looked at what he was pointing to. There it was, a ceramic lampstand that was a large red-and-white-striped lighthouse, and it was illuminating the room.

An Open Letter

Dear friends and family,

With a heavy heart, I write this letter to the family and friends of my son and myself knowing that it may cause offense. However, perhaps it may reach others in a positive way and make a difference in their life. If that is the case, then this letter will have been worth it to me as Randall's mother.

The medical examiner's office informed me that Randall passed away due to a drug overdose from fentanyl, a synthetic opioid. It is a powerful anesthesia used in surgeries and a painkiller typically for people with chronic pain (usually cancer related). It is cheaper for a drug dealer to manufacture fentanyl than the heroin or cocaine they put it in. The mixture of cocaine, alcohol, and fentanyl in my son's system at the time was a deadly combination. Drug dealers use this drug to extend the amount of product they are selling. When someone takes heroin or cocaine, mixed with this drug, they may not be aware they are taking something that is fifty times more potent than heroin.

This is important. When someone overdoses on fentanyl, CPR will be able to revive them. Medics and even heroin users use a drug called naloxone (Narcan) to bring someone back from a fentanyl overdose. If naloxone is not immediately available, the next best step is to use the Heimlich maneuver. The Heimlich maneuver can "mobilize" the lungs to breathe again to some degree. I am deeply grateful that someone tried CPR when Randall collapsed, but it was not the Heimlich and could not bring him back in this case. I would not have been able to save him myself had I been present because I was not aware of this fact about the Heimlich maneuver in this type of situation.

I believe in facing truth. I refuse to live a surface-dwelling life. This is another reason why I am posting this letter on social media. This drug is responsible for having killed over sixty thousand young people in 2016 alone. God help us. We have a literal epidemic on our hands, and we are losing so many of our precious young people's lives because of this.

Finally, I wish to express this: My son was responsible for a very terrible choice that took his life, and the individual or drug dealer who sold or gave him this drug was equally responsible. Because of this devastating choice on Randall's part, he took from me the joy, the laughter, the ups and downs in his future, the celebrations of life's journey as well as a possible daughter-in-law and grandchildren. Yes, I need to forgive him for this.

To the individual or dealer involved, you had a hand in ripping away the future of my son. Don't deceive yourself by saying to yourself, "I'm not responsible for Randall's choice." That is a dangerous half-truth. You were responsible for selling or giving away an illegal substance that brought about his death. Among those things also taken from me by you, I will not hear his laughter or his voice again, receive a Mother's Day or birthday card again. I cannot hug him, nor will I experience him hugging me again and saying, "I love you, Mom." I will not see or have opportunity to cherish and love any grandchildren in the future; he was my only child.

Nevertheless, I am praying for you. I will continue to pray for you. I purpose to include you in my prayers permanently, and I choose to forgive you.

Marguerite L. (Lever) Woodall

THE CONTROL FACTOR ILLUSION

Here I am again, expecting answers to relieve personal pain, stop all fear, and give me peace. In my devotional times, I try hard to listen for answers from God. Sometimes those answers come quickly but most often not. There is then the yearning and pursuit for answers in uncertain situations so I may somehow stay in control in this life. Hashing things out in my mind frequently gives me the illusion of control and makes me feel safe. Trusting in myself and mental analysis is not trusting in God, who is the answer. Few of us are comfortable with the unknown. Are you?

For me, the end result of trying to figure everything out ahead of time can end up in emotional and mental confusion that is never meant to be. Confusion is enemy territory. If the devil can keep you "chasing your tail" on an issue or event, he has accomplished his intent. As I pondered this subject one day, God spoke quite plainly to me about it. He said, "Because you don't have immediate answers, you walk away with no expectation of hearing one. This allows confusion to enter. Be patient. Wait. Keep seeking Me on the issue. Sometimes I hold back an answer for your sake. In due time, I will give it. Wait on Me in your heart, and I will speak My way in My time."

The greatest scientific minds have struggled with the concept of the existence of God because they trust in their own researched answers and knowledge. The result is that the fear of the unknown is held at bay, and greater still, facing any utter dependence upon an unseen God is then not necessary. Having to face the absence of any semblance of control in this life becomes unnecessary. For me, analyzing everything and every situation is common. I need to learn to let go and trust God for the answers that are important. In simpler terms, mental analysis can be self-protective to avoid feeling out of control.

I wonder if this is why so many seek the entertainment of the supernatural or witchcraft, which is so rampant in our time. It's all about the control over life because of the "power" presented. It seems to provide the answers some seek with their control intact. That illusion of control over the unknown causes them to come to believe that the answers to their questions lie in their own "perceived" powers. They become the answer, not God. The same can be said for those of us who follow Christ and demand answers to everything whenever we desire it.

We all struggle with trusting that there is a great and loving God at some point in our lives, especially when tragedy strikes. We are a fallen people, and we blame God for it and the end result. We tend to demand answers all the time. God cares, and He does give answers more than we know. We tend to miss God's response when we ask something because we don't know Him well enough to be able to perceive those answers when they come, or we are impatient. Our awareness of His presence is poor at best most often.

Another realization has brought me face-to-face with understanding that now, more than ever, I am alone. My son is gone, and so is his father, my husband, who died years ago in an accident at his workplace. He was a lineman and was electrocuted when inadvertently touching a power line. In the midst of this, there's more awareness of the fear of being alone in this world as well as learning to embrace the truth that we have little control of things in our lives.

Now I face these things in totality. We become so vested in our families and activities in our lives that this fear is not faced. It is good to be vested in our family and friends, and it is a wonderful part of relationship that God intends for us. However, if it all leaves us for one reason or another, we're left with facing this reality that has been there all along and not acknowledged it. We are alone, and it makes us feel out of control. Why? Because no one comes through for us as we hope for, at least not perfectly if at all. No one can fill us completely, and no one can love us in totality in every way because we are a fallen people. All the "stuff" this world offers us doesn't last long either; it's temporal.

I realize I have an opportunity here for greater spiritual maturity in this paradigm shift that has taken place in my life, and here's the paradox I also see: I must first acknowledge the loneliness that is very real in this world and the fear it produces so that I can embrace the truth that I am not alone because God tells me He is with me every day in every way. I don't like facing my fears, but it is needed if I am to walk in a deeper measure with the God who made me—who made us all. Of course, I could take another route and try to "cover over" the loneliness with someone or something else if I choose. So what do I choose?

I'm running…to God to learn more about Him, for Him to be more a part of me, to let Him hold me and love me as only He can, to embrace God as my great fortress and stronghold, where I am not alone, and it's okay if I'm not in control of my life most often. I can now begin to learn to live the rest of this life free of this fear of being alone and the need to be in control in an illegitimate way and learn to just be. Some call it "living in the moment."

It is then that I pray this: "Father, forgive me for avoiding the pain life hands me by demanding answers my way. You do provide answers in Your own way, in Your own time, not mine. Help me to be aware of Your responses to my prayers. Forgive me for seeking safety in my own answers instead of Yours because You are the answer. Help me to embrace the desolation in my life now and find You in the midst of it."

Trust in the Lord with all your heart,
And do not lean on your own understanding.
In all your ways acknowledge Him,
And He will make your paths straight.

—Proverbs 3:5–6

God and the GoFundMe

So many young people came to me to share about how my son had touched their lives. They came during the week of preparations for his funeral service, reached out in Facebook posts and at the graveside ceremony. Several stories were shared with me by his friends of how he stood up for those in school and in life who were enduring hardship and bullying. Randall was known for encouraging others who were downtrodden by life, and he readily impacted others with his infectious laughter. It had been life changing for some. He cared about the down-and-out, including those who were considered outcasts and unlovable. His favorite saying was, "If you ain't laughin', you ain't livin'."

My son had been slowly developing alcoholism and a growing drug addiction. I was aware of the drinking and partying and had hoped and prayed he would grow out of it as he matured as I had. I did not realize there was an addiction to drugs that had a grip on his life too. This was much more hidden from my view because I lived so many miles away in Oklahoma, and he was in Florida. He hid it well when we talked on the phone or we visited each other. In spite of this, he had impacted many. And I wonder what my son would have become had he lived, been free of addiction, and following God's direction in his life. He was gifted by God in reaching out to others with the ministry of encouragements and compassion and a laughter that brought friends an explosion of sunshine emotionally.

Randall had been visiting his grandparents in Florida briefly on the weekend of October 6, 2016 when he died. The decision to bury my son next to his father there was automatic, using the plot site that was originally intended for me.

Plans were made to fly to Florida with my sister the next day from Oklahoma. I was pondering how to pay for my son's funeral that I knew would be around $10,000. I thought about a Capital One charge card I had recently acquired. The credit limit on the card was $10,000, and I had set it aside for a planned vacation with my son to Rome. It was to be used strictly for unforeseen expenses or emergencies during the trip.

Initially, when I first received the large line of credit, it was a surprise to me as I didn't need a $10,000 credit limit, and I never dreamed of having to use the full amount. Now, however, it looked like it was my only option to pay for the funeral costs. Was this coincidence that I happened to recently receive a credit card with the same credit limit needed for the funeral expenses?

As I mulled over having to make payments on this card for the burial costs, I knew it would feel like a never-ending monthly reminder of my son's death as it would take several years for me to pay off such a large balance. Frankly, I did not know how I would be able to endure it emotionally on top of everything else for the long run.

The evening before our flight, my sister Mary approached me to share a very strong impression she believed was coming from the Lord. "Would I be open to starting a GoFundMe to help pay for the funeral expenses?" she asked. I was taken aback in that moment. I didn't think of God as a GoFundMe kind of God. Would He actually use a GoFundMe? I thought of this method of fundraising, as a whole, to be unreliable and might come across to others as desperate on my part in a tacky way (let's be honest here) because I'm a firm believer in being a financially responsible person, and I hate long-term debt. Truly, the credit card looked like my only option. However, who was I to say how God would choose to help me? I gave her my permission that night to start the GoFundMe, not really believing that it would be productive in any way, as I moved on to packing for the flight.

The next morning, and eight hours later, at our first layover in Atlanta, Georgia, Mary checked the status of the GoFundMe. To our astonishment, a $4,000 donation had already been made overnight, and more were pouring in. Donations came from people in every state my son had ever worked in over the years, which were from Tennessee, Washington, Florida, and Oregon; even former coworkers who were offshore on oil rigs in the Gulf of Florida donated as well. These were people whose lives he had impacted in his life journey through employment, high school, and the secondary education he had pursued. He had touched many.

The GoFundMe account hit $10,000 in less than thirty-six hours. The charge card with its large "unnecessary" credit limit was used to pay the balance due before burial. The funeral bill was exactly $10,000, and in turn, the GoFundMe released the donations three days later and paid the charge card balance off in its entirety.

I reckon the God who parted the Red Sea has no problem with GoFundMe.

Washington Friends

The Eye of the Storm

I t's the everyday things that God does to comfort us that we can miss if we're not aware. Indeed, God will lay a "groundwork" of comfort and direction ahead of time just before a tragic life event. During the months of June through September of 2016, I kept hearing repeatedly a new Christian song on the radio as I drove to work every day. It impacted me. You know, it was one those songs that sweep your soul upward in praise and hope toward God's throne room as you listen to it. I thought to myself, *This is an awesome song, and I love listening to it.* The lyrics drew me into worship every time I heard it. God's presence would surround me in my car as I headed to work when I sang along with gusto.

This song was called "Eye of the Storm" by Ryan Stevenson, and it speaks of being in the middle of the storms in life and how God continues to remain in control through it all. Even in the worst of circumstances, when life's storms rage around us, He is the anchor for our soul, and His love surrounds us to keep us whole. I thought about the many life events that have shaped my journey here on this earth as I listened to this song. I felt grateful for the faith God has been developing in my life. For me, life without relationship with Him is empty, vain, and aimless.

Yet again, I am reminded of another image that the Lord had given me about life's storms many years before. In it, I saw myself standing in the center of a tornado. The walls of the tornado were dark with dust, dirt, and debris as it rotated around me at a high rate of speed. The area inside this vortex was narrow, and I felt as though I could almost touch the wall of wind if I reached out. The middle area of the tornado was calm where I stood, and then I looked straight up to see sunshine and blue sky in the opening at the top. A silent understanding came from God about life's storms or tornadoes in those moments.

The message was this: There are multiple storms in our lives that we will encounter; some are very strong and can be destructive if we allow them to be. If we focus our vision on a storm's high winds and the dirt and debris swirling around us within its walls, it will pull us into it. However, safety, comfort, and peace in the midst of life's great storms come by looking up and focusing on the clear sky above—or Christ. Don't be sucked in by the visual around you or your circumstance; instead, "set your mind on things above" (Colossians 3:2). We often do not see where God is in our circumstance until after He has brought us through it. God is always in the midst of our storms guiding us through them to the calmer areas if we let Him. He prepares everything ahead of time, knowing what calamities will come. He will not leave any detail unfinished or any need unmet.

I requested this song to be played at my son's funeral service. I knew by then that God had highlighted it to me shortly before my son's death to begin to lay the groundwork of comfort and strength that would be needed before and after one of my life's greatest storms. He will use songs this way, and it truly helped to anchor my soul at that time. I have no doubt that it was a "message" from God sent ahead of time to prepare me. However, I found out later that there was more to the message than I knew.

One of the verses in this song speaks of a sickness taking a person's child away, and there's nothing a person can do but trust God in the midst of it. Months later, I sensed the Holy Spirit moving me to look more closely at the lyrics of the song again when I wanted to write about it here. I learned that a slightly different version was being played on the radio rather than the original. Only one line in the song was different. I was stunned and astonished when I viewed that original line that I had not heard before. Instead, the verse spoke of *an addiction* stealing a child away, not a sickness. This song's original verse directly spoke to the event I would be walking through months later with my own son dying of an overdose.

All through the Scriptures, the power of songs is very evident. Saul, a king of Israel, was plagued by a demonic spirit when he took his own rebellious course as king away from God. It was only David's singing to him that quieted his inner turmoil and drove the demonic spirit from him (1 Samuel 16:14–23). God commanded a king named Jehoshaphat not to fear when a large army was advancing against them and their city. Per God's direction, Jehoshaphat had singers with songs of worship go before his army to face their enemy encamped against them. It destroyed them all before they even arrived at the enemy camp (2 Chronicles 20:1–22).

Song is sometimes described as a vehicle of deliverance that God uses to give direction and comfort in the midst of the horrific circumstances that life can sometimes throw at us. More and more, I am hearing these "songs of deliverance" being sung by different Christian music artists in this day and time. These particular songs that are God inspired are "messages" from Him that are meant to communicate His care, guidance, and love, as well as preparation for future events. I am in awe of the God who goes to such lengths to reach us.

The message of this song, "Eye of the Storm," then became more relevant than I could have ever imagined. There are so many of us who have gone or are going through this particular life crisis, the loss of a child. This song of deliverance and comfort was meant for many, not just myself. But I wonder, how many have really "heard" it? How many others was this song written for by the living God? His efforts are real to reach out to those of us whose children are among the casualties of the massive drug addiction problem in this nation, and it is unwavering. How many will "hear" the message that is sent when there is the loss of children, friends, and family to other tragedies as well? Will they hear these songs of deliverance that are meant to comfort and encourage them? Is anyone listening?

Thou art my hiding place; Thou dost preserve me from trouble;
Thou dost surround me with songs of deliverance.

—Psalm 32:7

GOD AND THE FUNERAL SONG

The woman who stood before me, with her folder of sheet music, was volunteering to sing for my son's viewing and funeral. I had not met her before but learned that she was the mother of a young woman whom I knew my son had dated for several years. Randall and her daughter had cared deeply for each other. She shared with me in the course of our conversation something that I did not know. My son had attended church with her and her daughter during those years.

As a professional event singer, this woman's voluntary sacrifice was a tremendous gift from God that I had not anticipated. A professional singer for a funeral was an arrangement made typically by the well-to-do. Yet again, through the event singer's offer, another example stood before me of how God was stepping in to meet every need. My dear sister Mary, as an event coordinator in previous employment, had helped greatly with the various arrangements. Her presence and moral support were my bulwark. This offer, however, was above and beyond what I expected for my son's services. Everything I had forgotten to do or never even thought of because of the depth of grief, God had already taken care of. As He met each and every need that week, I was constantly being lifted and carried by His love through every moment.

As I thought of music that would be age appropriate and what my son would have wanted, the remembrance of the piano lessons I took as a child come to mind. I loved my piano. It was an old Ivers & Pond upright. Crafted from solid mahogany and embellished with ivory keys, I spent hours playing it and singing along to the sheet music given to me by my mother or my piano teacher. My mother even bought two huge Reader's Digest special edition books for me that were packed with decades of popular music for piano players.

I remember one piece of music in particular that stood out from all the rest. Being drawn to it frequently and playing it often, I sensed something powerful about it even at the age of ten until well into my teen years. The sheet music had a compelling illustration at the top of the page of a man walking a sunshine-filled path with his suit jacket slung over one shoulder and a peaceful smile on his face that was turned upward toward heaven. The name of the song was "I'll Walk with God" and was made famous by a movie called *The Student Prince* in the 1950s. The singer was Mario Lanza. In retrospect, I truly believe that this music piece was what started to draw me to Christ as a child.

This memory of being drawn to God as child through this music piece and my love for it was something that I had hoped to share with my son at some point in our future. I had never told him what had first drawn me to Christ. It was one of the many little things about myself that I looked forward to sharing with Randall in life conversations as we aged.

My son received Christ as a child, but when he became a young adult, he lived a life of excess in drinking and drugs. I had hope for a day when he would return to walking with God and forsake those things, and this memory of the music piece would be one of many to share with him that were a part of my personal journey and where it began. But now, this was not to be. I would never have the chance to tell him about these cherished memory things that would encourage him to follow God once again.

As I stood there, I asked the woman what type of songs she wanted to sing (I was secretly hoping in those moments that the songs were modern and upbeat). Her response was immediate, and it almost brought me to my knees as she pulled out a specific sheet of music, handed it to me, and proudly declared, "This was Randall's favorite!" I looked at the sheet music I was holding, and the song title read, "I'll Walk with God." Enough said.

He Grieves with Me

As I sat in prayer and study on a Monday morning, reflections of the deep pain that grief brings were coming to my mind. During the morning, as I take time to pray and listen to God, this grief comes and overtakes me. Grief has a mind of its own. I keep pursuing relationship with God every day despite the sorrow when it comes. On this particular morning, I sensed a movement of God's Spirit, so I sat quietly and opened my heart to just listen to what He wanted to say to me.

An image came to mind of Jesus sitting on the ground, holding me close to Himself on His lap. Others, on the dusty road where we sat, were passing by on their life journey. When I reflected on this image, I saw myself grasping His shoulder and burying my head in His chest, sobbing with grief as, for the first time, I allowed Him to hold me. He then began to rock back and forth, and I heard His loud cries of lament and grief for my son and me. He was impacted deeply by my pain, and His heart was broken too. I was stunned by the audible and very loud grief-filled cries I heard coming from Him. Then the image passed.

Others have testified to experiencing this kind of revelation. They speak of Jesus holding them closely when they are in pain, but I've never experienced God's holding me before, nor would I ever let Him do so. There has been a part of me that would not let God hold me when I've needed it most. Years ago, in my flight from God, I shook my fist at Him instead when He's tried to draw near or I sensed His presence.

During a Bible study hosted in my home at one time, the subject of demandingness was being examined. We demand that God come through for us the way we want Him to in our lives, and we become angry when He doesn't. This study required a self-examination to determine if demandingness was an ongoing problem on a personal level. I do not recall the question that was asked or the statement that was made one day during a group discussion, but I do remember my visceral reaction. The reaction I had and the words I spoke came so swiftly out of my mouth that it felt like a volcanic eruption. It seemed something else took over me momentarily, and I could not have stopped myself had I wanted to. My soul was engulfed in a deep-seated, long-buried pain, and I said, "What has God *ever* done for me?" The tone was hateful, resentful, and unforgiving. In that moment, the room was filled with silence. Truthfully, I was shocked myself at what I had said.

This incident began to bring a recognition that I had developed a lifestyle of being strong for myself over the years because of the abuse I had endured. *If I was not strong for myself*, I thought, *no one else would be.* There was a cold, defensive distancing that I used to protect myself in relationships from any appearance of weakness mentally or emotionally. I was committed to never being vulnerable again to anyone. As a result, I made *my* strength my god and was not allowing God to be my strength instead.

What I truly felt and believed in my heart had surfaced in that moment during that study. I believed that God had never come through for me or been there for me when I needed him the most in my life. For this reason, some of the scriptures in the Bible I have not understood beyond that of a historical context, especially when it spoke of Jesus's weeping with us and feeling our pain. The Scriptures say that Christ was a man acquainted with grief and sorrow, and I had just experienced a living demonstration of this through the revelation of the Holy Spirit as I listened and watched the heart of God for me. It was life changing. He held me, and He grieved with me—loudly.

I sat for several minutes in stunned silence, deeply touched and moved by the demonstration of God's love, care, and very personal concern through what He had shown me. I not only deeply felt His love, but I also heard it through His voice of grief for me in those moments. The God-inspired love for my son and me became reality because He grieved too, and it engulfed me. He felt my pain.

As I rose up to move on with the day's events some time later, I clearly heard a parting comment from God as I walked away. He said, "I will let your son know that you let Me hold you today."

July is Bereaved Parents month.
Artwork "Melancholy" by Albert Gyorgy
(On display in Geneva Switzerland)
Photo by permission of photographer Mary Friona-Celani

When Jesus therefore saw her weeping, and the Jews who
came with her, also weeping, He was deeply moved in spirit,
and was troubled, and said, "Where have you laid him?"
They said to Him, "Lord, come and see." Jesus wept.

—John 11:33–35

WHERE THE GOOD THINGS ARE

Have you ever wondered where the good things are? I think some of us come to the place where we've wondered if any good thing had ever been a part of our lives. Sometimes all we can see is what was not and could have been, as well as what is not now. It's as though all we remember are the abuses, tragedies, accidents, and failures that have been a part of our life journey. As I was driving home from work one evening, in the silence of my car, I was talking to God out loud. In reflecting on my life, I felt in those moments so empty and void of any positive movement of God's presence and direction for some time. Those feelings were coupled with the thoughts of a life that had been filled with seemingly nothing but criticism, verbal abuses, and hardships. It was then that I shouted out loud in the car, "Is this as good as it gets, Lord? Is this it?" I continued shouting this question out several times at God as I drove home. I was angry.

At the age of fourteen, I had tried to reach out to my dad one last time to connect with him as his daughter. After many years of trying to achieve his approval, what I received instead was the usual criticism of a supposed failure on my part. This had happened over and over again for most of my life. I turned slowly away from him in the middle of our conversation in the living room, walked into my bedroom, lay down on my bed, and cursed out loud the hope that I had had in even trying to reach out to him. Depression entered my life at that moment, and I could tangibly feel its presence. I had decided that hope was an enemy. It was then that a darkness entered my life in a greater way.

After my rant in my car, God brought something to my remembrance that He had shown me years before. In my early thirties, I had begun to follow Christ with much more earnest intent in my life. It was during a nap in the afternoon on one summer day that I was swept away in a dream about those very troubled teenage years of mine. As I slept, a "life review" of those years began. God's Holy Spirit began to reveal a great darkness, the darkness of rejection and relational abandonment by my dad in my life during that time period. It was all around me as I dreamt, and it felt like it was closing in on me.

The darkness was massive, and I could see no light. I was terrified, and I cried out loud in the room as I slept, "Lord, please stop showing me this! It's more than I can bear, and I'm afraid." It was in that moment, after I cried out, that the dreaming changed. I was suddenly remembering and viewing "good things" that I had had in my life at that time. God peeled back the darkness as the dreaming continued once again. I was swept up in an awesome, joyful recall of memories of those years that I had forgotten, and God thoughtfully paraded each scene in front of me in sequence. The darkness had overshadowed and hidden them from my memory all those years.

At the time, our family lived at the Wallowa Lake resort area in Eastern Oregon. At Wallowa Lake, the spring and summers were busy with vacationing tourists thronging the area. As the Lord guided me further through the dreaming, I saw my favorite shirt that I loved to wear that I had not thought of in thirty years. It was a white-and-purple-striped tank top (the colors stood out and were very vivid). Then I saw my favorite bell-bottomed jeans! They were all the style then. There were also the athletic shoes I had saved my money for to buy. The white suede shoes were styled with a patriotic flag theme of a red-white-and-blue flag design on the sides. They were my Peter Fonda *Easy Rider*-style shoes. I loved those shoes! The memory of my ten-speed bike that made me feel like I was riding the wind came into view. I had saved my money for some time to buy the bike. I saw Willie my horse that I had spent countless hours riding on the wilderness trails and around the lake area, its summer cabins, and streams. He was my escape from the volatile home environment during the day, and it gave me a wonderful sense of freedom for a time when I needed it most.

Russel's hamburger joint down the road was the source of the best milkshakes, ice-cream cones, or hamburgers one could buy. And the roller-skating rink just across from Russel's, built in large log cabin motif, was an evening gathering place for every tourist in the area of all ages. There was the large lake lodge, which was the stuff that movies are made of, and a marina with canoes and paddleboats for rent during the day as well as fishing for anyone who cared to try their luck. Many a summer day was passed swimming in the lake or just lying out in the sun for a while on the local water docks that dotted the shoreline.

The dreaming ended with a final memory and scene of the haze of smoke from the tourist's campfires in the evenings hovering over the area's tree line at the base of those majestic mountains as they cooked their meals. The smell of roasting hamburgers and hot dogs filled the air and drifted past our cabin two miles up the road.

I was shocked to have remembered these minor things from over twenty-five years ago and in such minute detail! They had long been forgotten. It was then that the dreaming stopped as suddenly as it had begun. The Lord had placed my family and me in an area that was one of His greatest jewels geographically. It was like living in Yellowstone Park year-round, and Wallowa Lake is known to this day as "The Little Switzerland of America." The fall season was stunning in color contrasts between shades of evergreen and orange. The mountains shouted out His greatness as the Creator. The winters were just as awesome with the deep snow that covered everything like a comforting blanket that settled on everything for a time.

It's beauty was awesome, and I realized in those moments that this wonderful place was a gift from Him in the midst of the abuse and darkness that pressed into my life. How blessed I was! He was there even in the middle of every dark moment. He had placed me there in my life journey for a reason. There were good things all around me that He had given even when I did not know Him. I learned that afternoon as I slept that He is the God of my past. He is the God who is the same yesterday, today, and tomorrow. He had made sure that there were many good things that were a part of my life during those years to counterbalance and buffer against the darkness and its chaos, and I am grateful for all those things.

The brief review the Lord walked me through in those moments as I slept also opened the door to more contemplation and reflection of those years in the months that followed. There were many other good things that were present during that time of my life that I had not thought about or really appreciated before. I began to see those years in their entirety from God's viewpoint and not my own, and my memories were profoundly different from that moment on because my perspective changed too.

A deepening thankfulness for what God had given me during that time began to grow in my heart. That darkness in my memories that I had felt for many years whenever I reflected on them was strangely gone, nor did it matter anymore. His light is all I can see now when I recall these years. I had been set free from the darkness, and an even greater gift came into my life after that: a thankful heart. A thankful heart enters into His presence every time.

No matter how desperate our lives may seem or how abusive the life journey has been, there are good things that God places along the way. He dances in our lives with the little things that are so special. They are easy to miss because we don't realize that He gives the everyday things that are a blessing: a favorite shirt, a bicycle, a horse to ride, maybe new shoes, or a good friend who walks with us. We often miss them because we expect the spectacular and obvious ones. Darkness begins to leave our lives when we adopt a thankful heart even in the midst of it all.

God does not fix things, though He could. But rather, in life's storms when they come, He's watching to see if we will draw close to hear His heartbeat and believe He has placed good things there just for us. Those things may be small, but they remain. I saw that His love placed them in my life to let me know that in the midst of the greatest hardships, He was there. Funny how all those seemingly minor "gifts" or good things can bring a fond smile and joy to my face when I think of them even now many years later.

As I awoke from my sleep, I sensed God's loving presence lingering in my room and a thick smell had supernaturally filled my entire bedroom also. I was astonished as I breathed it in. It was pungent, distinct, and unmistakable. It was the smell of campfires cooking hot dogs and hamburgers.

Wallowa Lake Oregon

Bless the Lord oh my soul; and all that is
within me, bless His holy name.
Bless the Lord, oh my soul, and forget none of His benefits;
Who pardons all your iniquities;
Who heals all your diseases;
Who redeems your life from the pit;
Who crowns you with lovingkindess and compassion;
Who satisfies your years with good things,
So that your youth is renewed like the eagle.

—Psalm 103:2–5

GOD AND CAPITAL ONE

I was a scared eighteen-year-old kid in 1974 who had left home to try and make it on my own and was hired off the street by a prestigious flower shop in the downtown area of Boise, Idaho. It was there that I received my design training from two master florists. For many years afterward, I've worked various floral shops in different cities and towns. I came to Christ while working at one of those floral shops in Corvallis, Oregon. The floral shop manager was married with two children but also lived a secret life of homosexuality. A young couple moved into his neighborhood one day, full of God's Spirit and grace, and led him to the Lord. I saw a deep change in a man who had led this alternate lifestyle for half of his life. I bowed my head as I sat alone at my kitchen table one afternoon and asked Christ into mine because of it.

As a florist, I've done two casket pieces for family members. The first one was for my son's father when he was killed in an accident on his job in 1988. Now, I chose to design the second one for my son. The funeral home graciously gave me permission to do this casket piece in their employee's break room the day before the viewing. At the same time, I had also notified my charge card company Capital One about possible large charges occurring from out of state due to anticipated funeral expenses so the company would not assume possible theft of my credit card or it's information.

As I stood in the flower shop, I wrestled emotionally on the inside about using this charge card and desperately hoped the expense would not be too large to pay off in a short period of time. This casket piece would easily cost $400 or more. As my sister Mary stood by me, I handed the list of flowers and supplies needed to the floral shop manager and waited for the bill total to be given. The manager understood that I wanted to design the casket piece myself. A few minutes later, she handed me her charges on a small slip of paper. The total was $149.60.

I was stunned. God had moved upon her heart to charge me for the cost and not the retail for them. As I stood there overwhelmed with God's provision in those moments, my sister had received a phone call from friends in Oklahoma as she stood next to me. They had called to express their condolences and to inform us that they had just deposited funds into my checking account for funeral-related expenses. The amount was $150. God had paid for the flowers twenty minutes before I had the chance to. God doesn't need Capital One.

But my God shall supply all your need according
to His riches in glory by Christ Jesus.

—Philippians 4:19

I pulled into my driveway in Tulsa, Oklahoma, six days later, having just flown back in from Florida. I remember feeling like I had barely made it through the previous week's events. The sudden death of a loved one causes immediate shock emotionally. Sleep is difficult for a time; there is a battle with fear in feeling like you'll never be able to handle everything; and your memory, long-term and short-term suffers for a while before it gradually returns.

On my front porch rested a large package that UPS had delivered while I was gone. I opened it after unpacking, and there it was, a beautiful and expensive grapevine wreath with dried flowers gracing its curves. Then it hit me: I had totally forgotten about taking home a live plant or fresh flowers for a remembrance from my son's funeral. In the same moment, the realization occurred that the airline would not have made accommodations for it either. I broke down and wept in awe, engulfed in the love of the God, who remembered this detail for me when I did not, the loving God who knew I could not have taken something onto the plane flight yet made sure that I now had a beautiful, cherished item of remembrance. My Father loves me, and He loves my son. And by the way, God will use Capital One.

On behalf of Capital One and myself, we want to extend our deepest condolences for the loss of your son. No words can take away the pain, but know you and your family are in our thoughts. Sincerely, Ana YOQ089

1·800 flowers.com

The Two Paths of Brokenness

I told God that I felt utterly broken with the death of my son. In these moments, I am aware of two paths that brokenness presents to us when tragedy or hardship strikes. We have a choice between allowing the brokenness to shape us into the image of Christ as greater intimacy with God is fostered through the hardship or choosing the second path, which reinforces a victim mentality and eventually propagates bitterness toward God and life in general.

We must ask ourselves the questions that no one wants to ask. Will the brokenness we experience lead us to a greater dependence on God? Will it lead to the permanent acknowledgment that our weakness prevails in this life, and only the Lord can be our strength? Will it break open our hearts to the point where we have dropped all pretense and learn to love others as we love ourselves? Will our focus shift to what really matters in this life and see it as Christ sees it? Or will one retreat into the bitter darkness of hatred toward God?

The first path can bring a new dimension to life right in the middle of all the pain. I had prayed for God to deal with my hardened heart several years ago when I recognized the issue. Now with my heart in a long-term state of brokenness, feeling other's pain washes over me swiftly when I hear of someone's suffering or distress. I am easily moved to compassion now as never before and even at times weep for them as well. Before I experienced tragedy in my own life, I displayed little sympathy or empathy for others. I never thought much about how others suffer through their own tribulations until now. Now, I choose to willingly express the emotions of sorrow and pain, to allow their flow in order to reach out to others who may be shattered by their own calamities.

The second path of brokenness can lead to a retreat in life. No one and nothing matters much anymore. We shove aside the tenderness of heart that the brokenness brings about and shut it out. The heart then hardens itself further and like prison doors, locks up tighter than ever against relationships, especially with God. Anger, depression, and bitterness progressively develop. The mentality of the "victim" begins to set in in our thought life. The "blame game," along with unforgiveness, eventually overtakes us, which we direct toward God or someone else. In short, we don't see a way out. The fruit of this path is emotional, relational, and eventually spiritual decay and deadness. This is the path of a fallen world's way of dealing with the brokenness when it occurs.

In the past, I've cared more about an animal that was suffering than a hurting human being. I say this to my shame, and over the years, while in prayer, I have told God that I knew there was something wrong with this attitude and that I didn't want to be this way. Human beings are supposed to matter far more than animals (and I deeply love animals). We tend to show more compassion toward animals than our own kind. People are higher in priority in God's eyes than His creatures. If we're really honest, I think many of us are this way but don't think about it much. This is changing now for me. Others do matter more. The death of my son had freed me from my bondage to a lack of concern for people. I now realize more than ever that I was a prisoner of my own indifference toward others. The love of Christ is beginning to prevail in my relationships, and it is a wondrous thing!

The first path is by far the best one and is the most fruitful spiritually if we choose it. Its fruit is *agape* love, self-sacrifice moved by compassion, and a helplessness that throws itself into the arms of God every day. A deeper territory of trust in God is entered into, and the spirit of grace manifests itself often. This is the path I choose.

If we allow God to take our brokenness and deepen our character through it in our lives and shun the world's way of dealing with it, then we have taken the right path. It is this path that participates in Christ's suffering, that leads to His holiness and the understanding of His heart and His heartbeat.

WHEN GOD GOES BEFORE YOU

After being off for two weeks for my son's funeral, I was back to work again. But my drive to and from work as well as my work days were now very different. I would weep as I drove into work and every evening as I drove home for several months. I often wondered if any other drivers on the road passing by might be going through a similar tragedy. Was there someone else also experiencing heartbreak as they commuted to work each day? Clinging to God became paramount in those moments, and I was so grateful for the foundation I had as a Christian when Randall's death occurred.

Throughout the days that I was at work, I would cry at the drop of a hat for any given reason at any given time. Yet in the midst of that, God was not finished speaking to me, not for some time. He would boldly yet gently and frequently reach out to me during my grieving in unexpected ways for many more months to come. In retrospect, I am amazed at how God, through other people, walked with me daily. God does incredible things for us in ways that we never expect them to happen. But we can only see them happening in our everyday lives if we chose to do so. He goes before us, sometimes months or even years ahead, to place people and circumstances in our paths to guide us through life's difficulties as they transpire.

I am not convinced that there is such a thing as coincidence because of that. He knows what will happen in our lives before they ever happen. After all, He is the alpha and the omega. And at this little grocery store I worked at, He had been there ahead of me. In fact, He has always been there.

My coworker Kay, who was assigned to my department to help me, was a petite spry woman in her early seventies, who was always on the go, the picture of health and vitality. Kay had been at this particular store location when it first opened, and so was I about twelve years previously. Grocery store chains often transfer employees periodically where the business needs them most. As events came full circle, I found myself in that same store location once again after having been transferred out several years earlier. Kay was there encouraging me daily as she worked with me. She listened to the heart of my grief and provided comfort in my sorrow when it would wash over me. Kay wept with me when I did as we stocked the store shelves together, and she walked with me.

Kay was a woman of God. Her husband died suddenly, years before, right in front of her as he collapsed on the front lawn of their home. At that time, Kay was still in her youth with young children. Even after her husband passed away, Kay never remarried. She was steadfast, positive, and faithful. I never heard foul words pass from her lips, nor did I ever see her involved in any usual gossiping. I felt like my spiritual maturity paled in comparison to hers in many ways. In her widowhood, Kay had been blessed with her adult children and grandchildren who carefully looked after her. I'm sure all of them hold her dear in their hearts, for she was a very caring and amazing woman.

There was a particular evening as I sat at home after work that I pondered the questions of "why." Why didn't God step in and rescue my son? Why didn't He send help at just the right moment? I've heard many miraculous stories of God's intervention in people's lives to save them. I was told that the paramedics kept missing the address they were called to when my son overdosed; because of that, precious time was lost. Why did that happen? Did demonic forces cause confusion and delay the emergency services, or was it simple human error? Did God chose to take away my son? Are there just foolish decisions that cause accidents that cost us our lives when we don't expect it?

The truth is, for those of us who have walked this journey, we dearly desire to have *those* particular "why" questions answered. I've been to several grief support group meetings as well as listened to scholars over the years who touched on the topic of sudden death and death in general. There seems to be a unspoken assumption that God will not tell us why. In some Christian circles, I've even sensed that we are not supposed to ask Him either!

It is often quoted that God moves in mysterious ways. This is a quote, I believe, that is innocently taken out of context and is meant to stave off any unanswered questions about the "why" to explain the seemingly unexplainable. Of course, in our grief, we do ask Him the question of why, but because of conflicting theological thinking or lack of deeper relationship with Him, we really don't expect God to answer.

At this point in time, all I knew to do was to trust God with the whys as I presented it to Him in my prayers that particular day and trusted that He would answer according to His will if He chose to. I chose to believe that He desired to answer my question about why He did not intervene and stop Randall's death.

That same morning, just after clocking in for the day, Kay walked toward me with a small scrap of paper in one of her hands. On the crumpled piece of paper was a handwritten scripture verse. She said, "The Lord told me to write this down for you and to give it to you today." The verse was from the book of Isaiah and read,

> The righteous perish, and no man layeth it to heart; and merciful men are taken away, none considering that the righteous is taken away from the evil to come. (Isaiah 57:1)

I immediately knew that the Lord had brought this message to me through Kay, and I wept. In my hand, I held a why question answered. That evening, as I walked in the front door of my home, my phone rang. An aunt of my deceased husband was calling. The aunt had reached out to me shortly after Randall's passing and had been calling occasionally to talk with me. I was still clutching in my hand that crumpled paper with the scripture on it as I held the phone to my ear. She began the conversation immediately by talking about a Bible passage she had shared with another family member that day in response to the question of why Randall died.

As she verbalized the first three words of the scripture passage, I interjected and finished it for her. I read it from the scrap of paper in my hand as the Spirit of God swept over me. It was Isaiah 57:1, and I was reading it to her instead! I heard a joyful shout from this woman as God's presence engulfed her and me both at the same time on both ends of the phone conversation. God was confirming His message first through Kay and then the family aunt to me.

There were several "messages" from God over the weeks and months that followed (those stories are to come). And God did give me more answers to the why questions; in fact, more than just one was given. He desires to give us those answers. We assume He doesn't want to give them. He loves us deeply and most often is more than willing to answer some of our questions we don't think He cares about. He is not a cold or distant God. If you've lost a loved one, do not assume God doesn't want to give you the answers you need. More often than not, I have come to expect answers to the hard questions in this life because those expectations are borne out of a deeper relationship with God. When you are close to someone, they want to respond to your questions.

If God holds back on an answer, it can be for different possible reasons. Yes, there are times when answers may cause harm if given to us before the appropriate time. It might be that our spiritual maturity needs to be greater so that we handle God's responses responsibly.

What I didn't know about Kay was that she had "walked with" someone else before me. It was a cashier who had also lost her son suddenly in an tragic accident. Kay had worked with her side by side as the woman walked through her grief journey. She cried with her as the woman grieved when they stocked the grocery store's shelves together also. It was no accident that God had given me someone who had a remarkable résumé in coming alongside another in walking through great pain.

God's timing by pairing me with Kay in my time of need was impeccable. Through her unbidden and on more than one occasion, He brought the comfort and answers when I needed them the most. Those answers came at the right time through a gentle woman coworker, just for me.

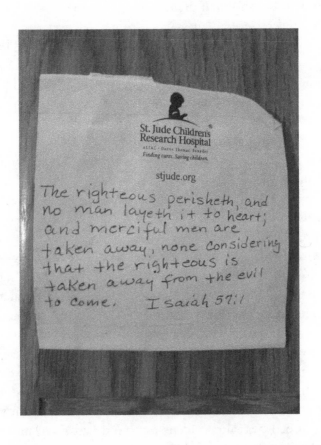

GOD, THE BANQUET,
AND THE FROGMAN

After watching the last of a video series at church about the family and its importance, my pastor asked us all a question: "What was supper like in our homes as children when we were growing up?" The supper table sets the tone for the knitting together of a family's relationships. Several people shared their experiences, and most were pleasant. I debated on whether to speak up at all on this issue. I chose not to.

As a child and for most of my adult life, coming to the supper table was an experience that was deeply dreaded each night. I remembered staying outside, playing as long as I could to put off coming inside for dinner when it was announced. As we sat to eat, the entire meal was fraught with verbal and emotional abuse and sometimes physical attack. My father did not hesitate to strike out at anyone during the evening meal. It was a nightmare. The best strategy was to just keep quiet, and perhaps one would be overlooked for any forthcoming abuse.

On the other hand, I have experienced a banquet with God in my life too. In the scriptures, God speaks of sitting at His table and dining with Him. Christ spoke of knocking on the doors of our lives and hearts, inviting Him in, and He would dine with us (Revelation 3:20). And yes, there is also the great banquet spoken of in Isaiah 25:6 after Jesus's return. The God banquet I was invited to and attended occurred in April of 1988. My son Randall and I were staying with my folks for a brief time in the Seattle, Washington area. My husband, Randy, was a lineman and worked frequently out of state. Our marriage was strained because of his frequent travel, and

53

I often felt like my son and I took second place in his life. We rarely saw him when he was home in between his jobs as well.

At the age of twelve, Randy had experienced a move of God while attending a youth camp. A deep conviction to become a minister of the gospel came to him. Out of fear, however, he did not follow through with God's plan. I had been praying for some time that he would return to God with his whole heart and follow once again.

Two weeks before his current job was due to end, Randy called me in the evening as he usually would. In the course of our conversation, Randy said to me, "Marguerite, I'm tired of living my life the way I've been living it. I want to know Christ in my life again. Can you help me?" I was surprised and ecstatic! This was an answer to prayer, a dream come true! Here he was, on the phone with me, voicing how God had turned his heart toward Him once again. Randy offered to quit his job early to join us.

I knew how much my husband loved his line work. With only those two weeks left on the current job he was at, I encouraged him to finish it and then return home. We discussed finding local work for him so that he would not be on the road continuously. In two more weeks, I thought, my husband would be back in our lives with a heart following God again. I could not wait! I was stunned and grateful, grateful that God had been moving upon his heart to return to a relationship with Christ in his life again.

During the night as I slept for the following two weeks, I began to experience visitations from the Lord. He was speaking to me nightly for long periods of time as I slept. They were lengthy conversations of some sort, but I could not remember what had been said when I woke the next morning. It baffled me. I knew that God was "downloading" something of importance to me that would be needed in the future. I had never experienced something of this nature and to this degree before.

What struck me the most when this occurred was the feeling that I woke up with. It was as though I had sat down at a great banquet all night with the Lord, and His words were feeding me as He spoke them. Each following morning, I felt a fullness and satisfaction that even now is difficult to describe. There was absolute contentment that came with it. It was the deepest, most profound satisfaction of spirit and soul I've ever known. This was an ongoing multinight banquet I attended in spirit and soul for those following two weeks as I slept. The impact of the nightly visitations prompted me to share the experiences with my mother. Needless to say, neither one of us knew what to make of it.

One night in particular, though, was different than the rest. In a dream, I was standing in a dark place. It was pitch-black. Then suddenly, a bright light came down on me from above, like someone on a stage when a light is turned on from above them. As the light hit me, I fell to my knees. In the light was the presence of God, and I could not stand before Him. My knees hit the ground like a sack of rocks. Indeed, I even shifted downward in my bed as I fell to my knees in the dream.

Two emotions ran through me at the same time as God's presence manifested in those moments. There was a deep terror or fear of God and at the same time, the love of God, which is not born of the human mind or soul. It startled me greatly. When I briefly woke up because of it, the same presence, for several minutes, was in my bedroom simultaneously as it was in the dream.

Two weeks later—on May 6, on the last day of the current job, and one hour before he would finally leave it behind—my husband died. Randy had accidentally touched one of the power lines he was working on and had been electrocuted.

As I sat in my parents' home later that May afternoon, I was brought the day's mail right in the middle of the shock and grief that had engulfed me and my family. Mother's Day was two days away, and Randy had sent cards and gifts ahead of time; there was one for my mother and one for me. In addition, there were carefully wrapped gifts for our son Randall for his upcoming birthday as well. All of these had arrived the same day and within hours of Randy's death and deepened the sorrow even more. At that time, Randy was thirty-four years old, I was thirty-two, and our son Randall was four. Up until that time, I had never faced the death of a loved one before, much less a sudden one.

As I entered the funeral home to make arrangements a few days later, I was asked if I wanted to see my husband's body to make sure everything was in order for the evening viewing that had been scheduled. I had dreaded this. I was facing death for the first time in my life and looking upon the face of someone I deeply loved. I entered the room where his body was and noticed immediately that my husband's face was very pale. There is a natural paleness from death, but this color was from a well-intentioned mortician's application of facial makeup that was several shades too light.

Randy was a deeply tanned individual. His blonde hair and blue eyes belied his American Indian heritage, which caused him to tan easily. I pointed this out to the mortician and directed him for several minutes on reapplying a darker shade of makeup so Randy would have a more natural appearance. I was guided by a supernatural calmness and peace that I had never known or experienced before. There was no falling apart emotionally and no fear for the twenty minutes of time that it took to reapply the facial color.

I walked down the funeral home's steps outside afterward to try to take in all that I had just walked through. The moment I stood in the sunshine on those funeral home steps, the content of God's nightly two-week visitations flooded my mind, and I remembered. The insight and understanding came to me that I had been through several "rehearsals" in my sleep from the Holy Spirit to prepare me for the twenty minutes that had just gone by. God had already walked me through it numerous times as I slept at night the previous two weeks before. He had been preparing me beforehand to be able to face my husband's death in His strength.

I knew that I would not have had the emotional strength and courage needed to walk into that room where my husband's body was if it hadn't been for God's preparations with me. The preparatory visitations of God sustained me through my first face-to-face encounter with death. The stunning encounter with God in the dream, where I dropped to my knees in holy fear, sustained me through the journey of my husband's death with the absolute truth that God is so very real and, above all, is love.

I will never forget the satisfaction I felt that surpassed any earthly ones that I've ever had as God spoke to me for hours on end while I slept. For a few nights over a short period of time, I dined at the banquet table of God, which was not filled with apprehension and uneasiness like the earthly one that I had known from my childhood. So when my pastor asked the simple question that he did, these were the memories that came to my mind. I've known both the table of love and the table of dread, and I look forward to dining at God's table of love in my eternal future again.

I'm sure you've wondered about the frogman in this story's title and where such a strange thing would fit in. My husband had the tendency to buy our son Randall the cheapest and cheesiest toys you can imagine in the airports and towns he traveled through over the years. It was just how he rolled. As I sat in the airport lobby waiting for the flight home a few days before the funeral, our four-year-old son skipped over to the nearby airport store a few feet away. I noticed a large fish tank in the store window with a battery-operated frogman figure dressed in diving gear, swimming around in it.

I saw my son's rapt attention as he was looking at it. It was really quite comical. Randall ran back out of the store to promptly ask me to buy the toy for him. It was difficult, but I had to tell him no. For the first time, he did not stomp his feet in protest as he would usually do. He had been rather spoiled by his dad on these types of purchases in the past. I was genuinely surprised that he did not pitch a fit but calmly accepted my answer instead. It was noticeable to me, and it struck me as very odd and out of character at the time, and I pondered why.

Randall ran back into the store to look around again. The second time he returned, he quietly sat down, and then a few moments later, he said, "Mommy, Daddy told me he loved me when I was in the store." I was dumbfounded and shocked! Then I broke down and wept. As he stood in the airport store again, God had allowed our son to hear his father tell him he loved him one more time. There was no doubt about that. As I grabbed my son's hand and headed for the store, I said out loud, "All right, George Randall [Randy] Woodall, I will buy our son the frogman." And I did.

REQUIEM FOR A FUTURE

B y far, the greatest challenge in my life at this time is looking for something to hold on to for the future. What was a large part of my life and future, my son, is now gone in a moment's time. Every life event that was yet to come with him has been canceled. One of the greatest shocks is when the future is immediately ripped away when a loved one dies. You know, the future events you have hidden in your heart for some time as a parent, waiting for them to be fulfilled. There's the expectation of your son or daughter falling in love with someone, becoming engaged, and all the joy and anticipation that comes with this significant life event. Who is this person who captured my son's heart? Do they know just how special he really is?

Then there's the introduction to this future spouse, their immediate family, and the developing relationships with these. Engagement parties are planned and then finally the wedding. Being involved in this culminating event of love would have been so wonderful. Would I have been asked to help plan it? How could I have helped financially and what kinds of wedding gifts would I have given that would express my deepest love for my son on this special day of his? I see myself sitting in the pew at the church, watching the wedding ceremony with tear-filled eyes and so full of joy to see him happy and in love.

Then there's children of my child, my grandchildren. How many would there have been? The first baby comes due, and I'd have already saved my money to be there to help in any way I could. It would have been amazing to share in my son's joy, to see his face when he holds his firstborn for the first time, then it's my turn.

The future birthdays with my son, his children, and his spouse; the holiday events, especially Thanksgiving and Christmas, that

I would've loved to be a part of—many years' worth in fact. Each grandchild's birthday gift I'd have picked out with loving care each year. Perhaps I would have lived close enough nearby so that fixing Thanksgiving dinner for everyone would be a yearly family event. I know that I would have made it extra special so it would not be forgotten and looked forward to for the years to come.

And then there would be those summers when I visit them, or they would visit me, and have all kinds of fun doing things together. The grandchildren's dances, sports, special events, achievement ceremonies, and finally, school graduations I would want to attend. Perhaps I would even get to see my grandchildren become engaged and marry themselves and hold these children too.

Then my life would come to a close. I could be so grateful to have my son with me who would walk with me through my final days, who would look out for my interests when this time comes, and my hope of leaving an financial inheritance for him. More importantly, and greater still, I'd have had the opportunity to impart a spiritual inheritance to my son and his family over the years, to be able to share the incredible life journey that I've known with the living God, with the view that it would guide his life's journey farther than I could ever go.

All of these things I have described will never be, and they should be. The immediate death of my future with my only child is beyond description. I feel like I'm totally blind and having to slowly feel my way along a long, high never-ending wall. I cannot find my future. A large part of my current and future purpose and identity has been ripped from me. How do I walk through this, God? I feel so lost, and I don't know what life events are left to me. I do not see or know my future now.

My son took some meaning to life with him when he died. Randall took my purpose as a mother with him into death. I certainly could not endure this pain without Christ's comforting me. Sometimes, it feels like no one cares about my situation. I don't blame them, though; they must move on with their own lives and not live mine. As for me, my life will never be the same without my son.

The future has been permanently altered. I realize now more than ever that I am alone. Does anyone know and see that I am alone now? With my son and husband gone, I have become much more aware of the fear of being alone in this world as I journey through it, and I'm having to face it now in its totality. We become so vested in our families and daily activities in our lives that we are completely oblivious to the concept of loneliness, and this fear is not faced most often. It is good to be vested in family and friends because this is exactly what God had intended for us. However, when tragedies strike and we lose our loved ones, we are left facing the aloneness that has always been there all along. It can be quite difficult to acknowledge it and move forward. The truth is we are alone.

We are alone because no one can come through for us as we hope for, at least not perfectly if at all. No one can fill us completely nor love us in totality because we are a fallen people. All the "stuff" that this world offers us doesn't last long either; it's temporal. I realize I have opportunity here to more deeply embrace what most fear to and to be able to find what is most coveted: a deep trust and intimacy with God in the middle of it all.

In the midst of the death of my future as I had anticipated it, I must first acknowledge the fear of being alone, which is very real. In turn, I can then embrace the truth that I am not alone from the biblical view, which tells me God is with me always. I don't like facing my fears, but I know it is necessary to grow and become more spiritually mature as I walk with God.

Of course, instead of facing the fear of loneliness, I could hide behind a disingenuous attitude or pretend it's are not there. I could even take another route and try to "cover over" the aloneness with someone else or something else if I choose. I'm choosing every day and every moment to run to God. Only He can bring me through the emptiness I now face. I want to live the rest of my life free of this fear of being alone. For this very reason, I want to learn more about Him, for Him to be more a part of me, to let Him hold me and my future, to love me as only He can, and learn to just be.

THE OAKS OF RIGHTEOUSNESS

To grant those who mourn in Zion,
Giving them a garland instead of ashes,
The oil of gladness instead of mourning,
The mantle of praise instead of a spirit of fainting.
So they will be called *oaks of righteousness*,
The planting of the Lord, that He may be glorified.

—Isaiah 61:3

Every one of us who follow Christ carry a God "message" to share with others. These messages are born out of life's events and how God impacts us. One topic that I've always been very drawn to in particular passages in the Bible are those that speak of the oaks of righteousness. They refer to the people who are fully committed to God in their lives, and the oak tree is a metaphor for what these followers are like in character.

Oaks are known for their great massive height and branch spread in their maturity as well as uncommon strength. Their roots run deep. They run downward vertically more than horizontally across the surface of the ground, and because of this, they do not topple easily even in hurricane force winds. Indeed, they can be a windbreak in front of something, like a home perhaps, where protection is needed from strong winds. I witnessed this in Florida many times over the years with incoming hurricanes. In seasons of weather-related distress, oaks will drive their roots even deeper into the ground below.

In contrast, a pine tree's roots, for example, run across the top of the ground horizontally; therefore, they are not "anchored" well in the soil, and they fold like matchsticks in high winds. I've witnessed this too. They are not deeply rooted in the ground to the extent an oak tree is. In times of unbearable seasonal heat, the shade of an oak can be a very welcome relief. Then of course, let's remember the birds of the air and other animals that seek shelter in its branches too.

The verse in Isaiah 61:3 speaks about these oaks, and it has stayed with me in my heart for many years. I have known instinctively that these verses were referring to my life journey as well as others in this time. It speaks of these oaks as planted by God to glorify Him. A people who would reflect the character of the living God because they have chosen to trust Him and to let Him shape their lives.

It was another two miles of driving before entering the local town where I lived to do my grocery shopping on this particular summer day. Suddenly, in a moment's time, the windshield of my vehicle disappeared as I was looking through it. In its place was what looked like a large movie screen, and I saw scenes played out before me as I watched. For the next few minutes, I wasn't driving my vehicle; someone else was guiding it for me. I've never had what is called an "open vision" before, but this was it, a vision that occurs when one is awake and "seeing" something in another realm while life continues in the norm around you.

The scene began with Jesus and I sitting on a fallen tree log on the top of a grassy hill overlooking a meadow in the distance, and we were conversing. Then the scene shifted suddenly, and I was standing on a hill overlooking the meadow itself. The meadow's grass gently swayed in a soft breeze, and it was filled with red and white poppies everywhere. Mountains surrounded the area in the distance all around. There was a solitary large oak tree at the far end of the meadow, and it was situated right next to a very deep, clear stream of water. I knew that the water was the source of the tree's incredible growth and size.

I found myself wishing I could stand under that oak, in its shade, and I immediately was. When the thought of being there had entered my mind, it became reality instantly. In a moment's time, I was supernaturally transported across the meadow and found myself standing beneath the oak itself. It was a massive tree, majestic and solid. Its shade was wonderful with the gentle breeze blowing through it.

As I stood there, I placed my hand on its trunk, and then another hand placed itself on top of mine. When I turned and looked, there was my mentor and dearest friend standing next to me, smiling. This woman had counseled me and been my teacher for many years in the ways of Christ and His kingdom. We had been through much together.

I looked over my shoulder back out over the meadow behind me from under the umbrella of this massive oak. Someone appeared seemingly from nowhere, out of thin air, and was standing in the meadow. Then another appeared and another until the entire meadow was filled with people. The first individual I saw was my dad. He was dressed in a purple sleeveless robe with a braided gold belt about his waist, but what stood out to me the most was a crown that he was wearing. It was solid gold, and its design looked like several thorn branches woven together. Everyone who appeared was dressed this way, and many more were coming.

At this point, the vision ended, my windshield returned to normal, and I found myself stopped at the traffic light that gave entry to the town I was driving to. I had just driven at least two miles and could not recall it. But some hand had guided my automobile safely down the road as the vision had played out before me.

In sharing this with my closest friends, some things were obvious in their interpretation, or so it seemed. Some of it I did not understand and could only guess. I understood that the purple robes the individuals in my vision wore represented the royalty or kingship of Christ. Gold usually represented deity in ancient times, and the woven golden crown of thorns that each person wore spoke of the divine quality of Christ in each person's life but not without persecutions. *Perhaps these were people I would meet in my future*, I thought.

Seeing my dad standing there in the vision brought to my mind when he had received Christ as a youth at a tent revival led by Billy Graham. However, in all the years of knowing him, he did not bear the fruit of Christ in his life and relationships. His life journey did not reflect the love of God in any way, shape, or form. I was troubled by that for some time and had been praying for him. This part of the vision, I believed, was a promise to me from the Lord for the future of my father, that he would return to Christ somehow and begin to bear the fruit of the Holy Spirit in his life as he had been meant to all along.

Amazing how a vision can be given, and in our shortsighted humanity, we expect immediate fulfillment. This is most often not the case. It was over twenty years later when I saw this promise concerning my dad come to pass. His diagnosis of terminal brain cancer had hit me hard. It was decided to bring our him to Oklahoma, where my sister and I lived to care for him in his final days. In my sister's home, Dad would be cared for until it came to the point where hospice would have to take over. I drove in from a nearby town a few times a week to help when I could. There was one particular day, however, when we needed someone to step in and watch him because we had many commitments between the two of us that we had to attend to.

A young woman named Christy from our church volunteered for the day to help our dad. When I arrived home at the end of that particular day, she was anxious to share about a very unusual occurrence, and a strange story unfolded. It appeared the Holy Spirit had visited our dad during our absences. She excitedly described what had transpired. Talking was difficult for dad as the cancer had overtaken his speech center. Turning to Christy at one point, he indicated he was thirsty. "Can I have a drink?" he said while halting and stumbling in his speech and gesturing with his hands to indicate his need. "Can you fill my cup?"

Christy immediately assumed he wanted more apple juice and asked if that was what he wanted. "No," he said, "water of life." In that moment, Christy realized Dad was thirsting for something spiritual that only God could bring to him. He was thirsting to be filled with the Living Water, God's Holy Spirit.

It was then that she laid her hands on Dad in prayer, and the power of God's Spirit came upon him and filled him. Shouts of praise, adoration, and worship began to flow from his lips and reverberate throughout the room. He was shouting out in exultation some of the different names and titles of Christ as he worshiped God on his deathbed. His voice filled the room with biblical praises for Christ.

Christy quietly exited the room, she said, closing the door, and left Dad with God's presence filling him and the room. It was a divine and private time between him and God. The words of praise she described to me were ones that I'd never heard him speak in my entire life and which were completely out of the character for him in the past. It was the baptism of the Holy Spirit.

Though my dad had received Christ as a youth, I do not believe he was ever filled with the baptism of the Holy Spirit. It is the Holy Spirit that causes us to bear the fruit of the love of God in our lives. I know my dad watched my journey following Christ over the years. He didn't say much about that. I do know he saw in me a steady consistency and commitment even in the midst of very trying times and tragedies that would have turned most away from God. My dad had asked for the water of life because he was thirsty spiritually, and he knew something was missing. God met him in that bedroom and filled him. And there it was, the fulfillment of the vision concerning my father from twenty years ago.

As he lay dying a few days later, he told me how proud he was of me, which was something I had never heard before as his daughter. My father had endured tremendous persecutions because of his father's cruelty to his own children as they grew up. Maybe those were the thorns of persecution in his life, represented with the crown of woven golden thorns. The abusiveness has been generational.

I've moved in with my sister and her family temporarily after my son died and five years after our dad passed away. Here I sit, in the same bedroom where my dad was dying and worshiped God on his bed. In this small bedroom every morning before I go to work, I spend time with the God I love. Even sitting here now, His presence sweeps over me as I write this, and tears are streaming down my face. The irony just can't be ignored.

But what about the rest of the vision? Some of it, I had understood; however, some of it I did not. Recently, the Lord "corrected" me on the interpretation of the vision from so many years ago and the understanding I did not have before was given.

The tree I saw was not the tree of life; it was an oak of righteousness. The deep crystal clear stream next to the tree was the Holy Spirit's living water that the oak was feeding on for growth and life. My mentor and teacher had a hand in planting this tree in the good soil next to the best source of water available. The placing of her hand over mine on the trunk of the tree was the acknowledgment of what her teaching and mentoring would eventually accomplish in my life. All the people continuously appearing and filling the meadow were those who, in the future, would look for the shade, strength, and shelter the oak was meant to provide in difficult times, which is what it had been planted to do. Astonished, I realized that the oak tree was me.

This is my message: Let God bring the changes and growth in your life that are necessary so that you become a steadfast, mature Christian who gives shade (relief) and comfort to those in need. The end result is that you will become one who emanates the strength of God to those around you because you are deeply rooted in Christ, and your growth comes from the streams of the living water of God's Spirit, whom you have chosen to draw life from.

Are you a tree?

How blessed as the man who does not walk
in the counsel of the wicked,
Nor stand in the path of sinners,
Nor sit in the seat of scoffers!
But his delight as in the law of the Lord,
And in His law he meditates day and night,
And he will be like a tree firmly planted *by streams of water,*
Which yields its fruit in its season,
And its leaf does not wither;
And in whatever he does, he prospers.

—Psalm 1: 1–3

Jesus and the Justice Economy

My dad was what is referred to as a critical alcoholic. My siblings and I lived daily under the constant gaze of contempt and intimidation. He ruled the household with intense fear. The critical remarks and disdainful attitude were a constant of life. If I tried to engage my dad in conversation, I risked being verbally stripped of my dignity and left bleeding to death emotionally because of his searing derogation and contempt. Nevertheless, I tried over and over again for several years to talk to my dad about life and everyday things to connect with him. The result was always the same; it never wavered.

As I entered my early teenage years, I stopped trying to engage my father in conversation. I did so only if necessary. His god was his intellect and his collection of facts and knowledge that gave him a superiority over others in relationships, which, ironically, also cut them off. We never connected as a father and daughter because of it. No thought or idea that I had was worthwhile but rather was treated with utter contempt and scrutiny. Nothing was good enough.

I sat quietly and listened intently to the speaker on the stage. I had been here before at this type of conference with the gathering of different Christian denominations. The man on the stage was speaking on the subject of unforgiveness and the resulting "justice economy" that we tend to operate in in our lives as a result. The "justice economy" presupposes that those who have wronged us in any way must "make it right" or "fix it" through some form of payment that we have determined will satisfy us and smooth things over. We want people to use the currency we have determined will best meet the need for the perceived injustice that was perpetrated, then we can move on. Hearing the words "I'm sorry I hurt you" or "I'm sorry I abused you. Can you forgive me?" fit well into the currency of the justice economy.

Sitting there listening to his words, I mulled over the emotional demand I've lived with and been aware of most of my life and never understood. Having prayed about it often, I had no real answers until these moments as I sat and listened to this particular speaker. I've always had the deep sense of a need for justice, for things to be "made right" in unjust situations. It would manifest itself in my life when looking upon the injustice perpetrated against others and of course myself. The anger and, at times, the rage due to any injustice would express just how deeply painful it is. The helplessness one feels can be off the charts. Why was this issue such an undercurrent in my life? I had had no answers or resolution until now.

The conference speaker on stage handed a man in the audience three coins and then said, "Now, I want you to say something to insult me. Say something to me that is hurtful," so the man did. The speaker staggered back with a hand on his heart in exaggerated and feigned hurt and then stuck his hand out and said, "You must give me one of those coins to pay for the insult you've spoken to me." The man handed him one of the coins. This scenario repeated itself three times until the man in the audience ran out of money. There was no currency left to compensate for the next insult the man in the audience was prompted to speak again. When asked for payment by the speaker, there was none. There was no payment to be had and that just wasn't good enough.

As I listened, the Lord brought to my mind an image He had shown me many years before. It was an image or picture meant to explain the damage done to my heart by my father as a child and as an adult. In it, I saw my dad standing in front of me with great anger painted on his face. With my heart in my hands, I lifted it up to him to share it with him as his daughter. Instead of receiving it, my dad took it, threw it to the ground and stomped on my heart as hard and as forcefully as he could. My heart was on the ground between us, crushed and collapsed and beaten to a bloody pulp.

In the minutes that followed, as I sat there seeing the image again, I saw Jesus Himself walk into it as the speaker on stage finished. He stood beside me with both of us facing my father together. My heart was still lying on the ground, crushed, and He leaned over to me and gently whispered in my ear as we stood side by side and said, "Was it good enough?" I knew immediately He was speaking of the sacrifice of his own life so that my father could be forgiven for what he had done.

As Christians, we are taught that Christ covers all of our sins when we receive Him. In the Father's eyes, Christ's sacrifice was good enough to "cover" me. His justice economy had covered my sins. He had paid the price. But what about the others in our lives that have hurt us so deeply? The tendency is to forget or be shortsighted about the fact that Christ sacrificed Himself for those who hurt or abuse us too. I realized in those moments that my understanding of salvation was self-centered. The currency of Jesus's death had covered my sins by paying the price, and I had not thought beyond that. Now, it wasn't just about me anymore.

The question came to me quietly again: "Was it good enough?" Was the currency of His sacrifice enough to cover my dad's sins also? How could I tell Jesus, as He stood there in that image, knowing about the horrific death He endured, that it wasn't good enough?

With both of us side by side, staring down at my brutalized heart laying on the ground, I whispered back, "Yes, Lord, it was good enough." I walked quietly out of the image and forever left it behind; now that is the best kind of justice.

> For Christ died for sins once for all, the just for the unjust,
> in order that He might bring us to God,
> having been put to death in the flesh,
> but made alive in the spirit.

> —1 Peter 3:18

The Last Thanksgiving

My dad struggled to eat at the family table this particular Thanksgiving holiday. As I helped him to do so, I reflected on many things. He was slowly dying of brain cancer. After a terminal diagnosis, he had to be moved from his home in the Seattle, Washington area to my sister's in Oklahoma so we could care for him in his last days. At times, he fought our attempts to help him. Dad was a proud and independent man. Of course, the brain cancer had greatly affected his judgment about his situation too. For a time, he genuinely did not believe he needed anyone's help or intervention.

I've thought much about his life and growing up with him as his daughter. He was a cruel man and arrogant. Criticism was second nature to him, and it ruled his thoughts, words, and actions on a personal level constantly. The profound damage done emotionally to me and my siblings haunts us to this day. If I could put it into one word how he made us all feel, the word would be "rejection." I'd stopped talking to my dad years ago as a young teenager. Any conversation with him was dangerous emotionally for fear of the caustic criticism that would spill out. Sometimes, I felt like one more demeaning remark from my dad would be more than I could bear.

I kept trying to keep my dad's spoon upright as I helped him eat the holiday turkey and dressing. In retrospect, God has brought me far in my life's journey. One of the worst prisons in life is unforgiveness. It can disrupt our path of life greatly. Through Christ's strength, I was learning to forgive the abuse of the past, and as I sat at this table of Thanksgiving, a sadness overcame me. I reflected on what could have been in his life and the lives of those around him had he not been verbally and emotionally abusive. Few family members knew that he had been called into ministry after his initial salvation experience as a young man. He had never fulfilled it.

My walk with Christ has been tremendous in helping me to overcome the emotional and spiritual harm caused by the abuses I received at his hand. As Christian people, my sister Mary and I had decided that honoring a dying parent would involve caring for him in his last days despite the past hardships of relationship that he had caused. It was incredibly difficult for Mary during those few weeks as he repeatedly got out of his bed and fell during all hours of the night. He was gradually losing his speech and his mobility. Driving from work to help was hard for me as I lived several miles away and could be there only once or twice a week.

Through all of it, I frequently found opportunities to tell him how much I loved him without the fear of being verbally rebuffed as usual. During his final days, my dad could not voluntarily choose to back away or verbally retort in return. He couldn't stop me or interrupt with criticism because the cancer was slowly draining away his ability to speak. Now, I was no longer afraid to tell him the words of love regularly during conversations with him. I could finally enter his life with the love of a daughter and of God. For the first time, my father told me how proud he was of me before he ceased speaking altogether.

I cannot begin to describe how liberating it was to honor him even though everything in us and the world says not to! To love is to honor someone regardless of their actions past or present. God's love sees the potential of what now is (regardless of the past) and what can be in someone's life. My father asked me one day if I would be with him in heaven, and I told him, "Yes, Dad. I promise you, I will be there!"

It was a Friday morning on February 21, 2013, and the time was 12:50 a.m., and I sat by my dad's bedside and held his hand as he passed on. My father tried to tell my sister and me to leave the room as his final moments came. Perhaps he believed he deserved to die alone. I had already made the decision that no matter how abusive he had been, he did not deserve that. It was awful witnessing his passing. Death is ugly. In those moments, as his spirit left this world when he took his last breath, I spoke out and said, "Daddy, Daddy, Godspeed, Daddy. God is with you!"

There are many "cancers" in this life, and one of them is unforgiveness. I am thankful that God has forgiven me for many things and is teaching me to also forgive. Because of this, I could enter my dad's life one last time to honor him and love him as I had always wanted to but could not. We all die, but so few of us live well in the midst of our pain.

The Holiday Voice

I've been pondering another reason why holidays are so difficult for those of us grieving the loss of someone we loved. There are the obvious reasons, of course, which include the fact that they are not physically present anymore. They're nowhere to be found, and that's hard enough. The holiday occasions represent joy, celebration, and a deepening of relationships. We *remember* each other with a card or a call. The celebration, unfortunately, for those who are grieving, points out the empty spaces or places once occupied by our loved ones. The obvious becomes a glaring reminder.

A couple years later after Randall's passing and just a few days before Christmas as I slept one night, I dreamed of the time I'd be spending with my family nearby at their house for the holiday. All was well, and the celebration was such a wonderful time together until I had to go home later that day. I literally started weeping in my sleep as well as in the dream as I realized I was going back to an empty home and what felt like an empty life. My son wasn't there anymore.

In the midst of later reflection, the one thing that stood out to me the most is the voice that God gives us and its impact on those around us in our lives. It communicates life from the person it comes from. The expression of a person's voice is the audible evidence that that person is alive and present here with us. When my mother passed, I was so lost for a time not hearing her voice in the weekly phone calls she would make. It just suddenly stopped.

A year after my husband died, I struggled to remember what the sound of his laughter was like. There's a God-given mechanism that blocks some memories for a time when death strikes, especially sudden death, until some of the grief passes. It is like a long-term shock that slowly and progressively wears off when you are at a place that you can handle the return of intimate memories of the loved one who was lost.

I couldn't recall what my husband's laughter sounded like. Some time had passed, and I was at a place where I wanted to remember. I wanted so much to hear it again, yet I could not recall the memory of Randy's laughter. As I stood in my home one particular day, I prayed and asked God to restore the memory of my husband's laughter again. Immediately, in that moment, God released a memory of my husband sitting on the living room couch, laughing out loud uproariously. It was awesome! At the same time, I was relieved that the memory was still there.

More than anything for me, it is the voices of the loved ones that are missing that hurt the most. There was an emptiness in my life when my mother's phone calls stopped. There is a part of us expecting to hear that voice again, but we no longer hear it anymore. Our voices are one of the biggest indicators of a person's soul that is present and living life.

I don't hear my son's voice here anymore. As a follower of Christ, I know that I will hear his voice again, and we will be speaking daily and laughing often for an eternity.

Is There Room at the Inn?

During the Christmas season—with the story of Jesus Christ's birth abounding everywhere, especially in church culture, as well as all the holiday celebrations—a different thought came to me in the midst of it all. Jesus's parents were turned away at the local inn when they sought shelter just before His birth. The proprietor of the inn explained that the inn was completely full, and there was no room left. The innkeeper didn't know that the Son of God was about to be born. He had no idea who he was turning away at the door.

For those of us who are followers of Jesus Christ, I wanted to ask this question: do we invite Him in to occupy and fill every room of our hearts with His presence? Our hearts have many "rooms" filled with "stuff." You know what I mean, those things we want to keep and refuse to let go of. These rooms are full of us: our goals, our pain, our plans, our ways, and our desires.

When Christ comes to the main entrance of the doorway of our hearts, seeking to occupy the rooms within, and He is pregnant with His kingdom and it's power, which is meant to give birth in us, do we send the "innkeeper" of self-interest to answer the door to tell Him that there's no room at the inn?

GOD AND THE ARMS
OF COMMUNION

I sat in the chair in the sanctuary, staring at the church Christmas tree that night. It's height almost touched the ceiling. Two months had now passed since my son Randall's death, and I found myself getting ready to take communion together with my pastor and his wife. It was our pastor's tradition to do so with each individual family, single person, or persons on Christmas eve. There was a minute or two of remembrance of what Christmas was all about; sometimes a prophetic word would occur, then the partaking of the bread and wine.

My thirty-four-year-old nephew insisted on taking communion with me this night. As a struggling addict himself, he was reaching out to me in my darkest hour. He was in disbelief that he had not died first because of his long-standing addiction but my son had instead. I appreciated his gesture of comfort and support. I knew his heart was breaking also for me.

After taking the bread and wine of communion with him, he turned to me and said, "Auntie, I saw a second pair of arms and hands running parallel on either side of mine. There was the bread and the wine in either hand too. The arms and hands were taking communion at the same time as I did."

I understood in that moment, that he had seen something spiritually, a glimpse through the veil, and the unseen was allowed to be seen. He had not expected this, and it surprised him, and I felt he might have been unsettled by what he saw at the same time. In an effort to reassure him I said, "It must have been the arms of Christ taking communion with you, Jon." This was, of course, my first probable explanation.

But he firmly replied, "No, no, Auntie. They were Randall's."

It occurs to me now, two and a half years later, that my son was also taking communion with me.

THE WAILING BENCH

The only way I've made it through this "parents' worst nightmare" was because of a solid foundation in my belief system in Jesus Christ and staying focused on Him. Where my strength failed me during this event, God carried me completely through. Though I live out of state from where my son died and was buried, a dear friend bought me an airline ticket and flew me to Florida to stay with her where she lived also so I could visit my son's grave site for the first time since he had passed. It was almost two years later. This was my time to finally face more deeply my son's death that I had not been able to before because of the prevailing shock and having to return home so quickly afterward. I knew this day would come with God's leading. It was needed, and it was time.

My son was known for saying, "Real men can wear pink!" He was muscular from frequent weight lifting and all man, and he would deliberately wear pink shirts at times just to tease his many friends and prove his point. I guess he wanted them to know that his masculinity wasn't dependent on what colors he wore. These friends had placed pink roses on top of Randall's burial site periodically in remembrance of him in the days that followed, and it was now my turn to bring my pink roses. It meant everything to me to be able to bring my bouquet of flowers and to lay them down on his grave, to express the deep, heartfelt love and grief for a lost son.

Before flying out, I shared with my friend in a phone conversation that there would possibly be a moment for me when we went to the cemetery together to finally be able to enter into and then release some of the deep pain that was buried within me. I asked that she not comfort me if that occurred. Comforting someone can, at times, hinder a work God wants to do in our lives rather than help. My goal was to trust Him in the midst of the pain and sorrow no matter how terrifying it would become. The deeper pain had surfaced briefly on one occasion, and in that moment, I had felt an overwhelming suicidal urge trying to engulf me. I stood my ground in Christ at that moment, and it passed.

I was hoping for a release of this pain not only of my son's death, but many other lifetime events that had brought sorrow, sadness, and hardship in my life that I had not let go of and through stubborn pride had stuffed them deep down inside of me, locked away for many years. An unspoken vow in my heart, which I had made years earlier, kept me a prisoner emotionally. "I will never be hurt like that again," I had promised myself. The end result from this vow was that I had locked myself in on the inside from feeling any deep pain ever, and I could not pass through my self-imposed prison doors to really live and feel deeply. It would take the living God to break me free from my self-imposed imprisonment. I could not do it with my own strength. The provision of the airline ticket was from the Lord for me to not only walk farther in my grief journey to complete what I could not on the day I laid my son to rest but to also set me free from the pain of my past.

Now that there were no crowds, I could finally mourn openly and deeply at the cemetery. When my friend and I arrived, I laid the bouquet of roses down on Randall's grave, walked to the nearest stone bench a few feet away from the headstone, sat down, and wailed loudly. I was told afterward that the sound of the lament that came from me was a very deep and long one. A close friend of my former husband also came by later that day to the cemetery. There were photos and mementos I had wanted to give him for some time that had belonged to my late husband. They were the closest of friends for many years previously. We hugged each other and chatted for a time, reminiscing about days past. A few hours later, my friend and I returned to her home.

I do not remember a single hour spent at the cemetery that day—none of it. After I had purchased my pink roses for the graveside site and as we began the drive to the cemetery across town, I entered into a darkness for several hours of my life that day, and I had no recall of the events. My friend recognized that something was terribly wrong as I walked around during that time period among the headstones. She began making phone calls to friends and family for direction on what to do as she and I walked around, lost. She knew I was "not there." My sister suggested the possibility that I might be experiencing an amnesia-type episode due to possible shock. To her credit, my friend followed the events without interfering and let it play out, and afterward, she drove us back to her home.

The pain that needed to come forward from my heart, the pain I needed to enter into, was so deep, it caused an amnesia or possible disassociation that lasted most of the day. After returning to my friend's home that afternoon, I came out of the darkness and returned from the other side of the pain. As I sat down in her kitchen area when we returned late in the afternoon, I said, "I'm back now." As I spoke those words, it was as though I reentered into the present moment, not knowing where I had been for several hours. I was aware of my surroundings once again (much to my friend's relief).

Entering the deep pain of my loss was, for me, walking through a type of the valley of the shadow of death and trusting God that I would come out the other side of it. I had made up my mind that I would face it and walk through, and I chose not to be afraid.

It has been four years now, and I still do not remember what occurred during those hours at the cemetery. I knew that by accepting the airline ticket to visit my son's burial site, I had chosen to trust God with my agony and pain and a final goodbye. In those moments, I trusted Him even in the midst of my mind's failing me in the deep sorrow. He led me through to the other side of it. I had trusted Him to be my light of navigation and that He would take care of me even though I didn't know who or where I was for an entire day, and He did just that.

It doesn't really matter that I don't remember what transpired on that day. What God wanted to accomplish had been done. In the deep, wailing bellow that came forward from me, there was release and healing, and I trusted Him with my life more deeply in those moments. He will return any memory of that day if and when He chooses. I have trusted Him with that. I was finally free from my self-imposed, emotionally dead prison. We are all "runners" in this life. We run from discomfort and distress frequently through many avenues, such as drugs and alcohol. I have learned not to be afraid of hurting and to hurt deeply; life is painful at times. Pain can drive us to deeper intimacy with God if we allow it to do so. It also teaches us compassion for our fellow man, and that compassion can move mountains in others' lives.

The Valley of the Shadow of Death is not just the experience or journey of those who "pass over" when they die, but also the experience emotionally of the ones left behind that loved them.

—M. Woodall

DEAR READER

April 10, 2019

It is here in my journey that I wanted to write a personal letter to those who have been kind enough to read this book. Two and a half years have passed now since my son died, and it has been very hard. Sometimes, I have felt like I would not survive.

A year and a half later, following my son's passing, I found a lump in one of my breasts, and it was cancer. I could legitimately say that I felt like everything but the "kitchen sink" was being thrown at me in life! Now, on top of the grieving that ebbs and flows through my days, there was the fear of my own death that I've had to face as well. What do you do? Did I forget to mention the death of my husband when our son was four years old? I was widowed at the age of thirty-two. There was the sudden death of my mother on a Mother's Day weekend when I was in my forties.

My dad passed from a brain cancer five years previously. I watched him die in front of me. Even though this man was cruel in almost every way, no one deserves to die alone, and I chose to stay with him as he passed. It was difficult. The hope for a normal relationship between a father and daughter was now lost, at least on this side of heaven anyway. During the minutes that followed his death, I thought I would lose my mind as I reflected on what I had just experienced. It was then that a hospice pastor, who happened to be present, walked me through those moments afterward. Once again, God placed the right person there at the right time to help me through emotionally.

The message here is not how much I've been through. I am not a victim. Many have and are going through much, much more than myself. What I want to convey is the importance of having deep roots in Christ, a relationship that sustains and carries us through every hardship. I would not have made it through without faith or trust in a living God who cares for me and for all mankind. It's easy to become angry with God when bad things happen, but then I recognized long ago something that many Christians and people in general do not see. They think they do, but they do not. They live in a world they have created mentally that is meant to insulate themselves from harm or emotional upset of any kind (which I have done myself, by the way). Those internal, mental "worlds" that occupy our thoughts do not allow for bad things to happen on any given day.

So when tragedy strikes, we are taken completely off guard, become angry at God, and then we walk away. What was missed? How was our thinking flawed? This one truth has typically not been faced. The truth is this: we live in a fallen world, and it will not be restored until Christ returns. In our way of thinking, there's the presumption that all will be well all the time here and now. The Lord set me free of my "Cinderella" world, as I called it, many years ago (which is a story for another time). Like Cinderella, I was waiting for that knight on a white horse to rescue me from all my troubles. We must come out of the "worlds" we've created for ourselves so that we can live well as Christ intended for us to. God wants us to be kingdom minded people.

This is my message to the world. When you are walking with Christ, there will be change that must take place. It is change of thought, character, and direction in your journey. I am an agent of change. For many, for one reason or another, this has not been the case after they came to Christ. As a result, the world beats you up at every turn, and you do not understand why.

I want to also share about a facet of my grief that is really quite amazing. The death of my son has driven me into a deeper relationship with God much more than I have ever known. I've had many defensive walls up in relationships in my lifetime as well as a hard heart for many years. The breaking of my heart because of this event opened me up to receive and, more importantly, to flow in the godlike love that is spoken of in the Scriptures that God gives freely if we ask. I had no understanding of the love of God and what it looks like. The "crushing" of my heart paved the way for a softened one, and the humility needed to flow in His power and love and not my own. In our brokenness, God moves deeply if we let Him.

The deep, incredible change that has occurred in me, and continues still, is nothing short of a huge paradigm shift in my character and worldview. Don't get me wrong, the changes have been occurring all along in my journey with Christ; however, the death of my son was the earthquake that brought a brokenness to me that took me beyond myself and into utter abandonment to God and His plans for my life.

I have prayed for many years to be a person with Christlike compassion. As a result, when someone's misfortune presents itself to me now, I weep for them too. Before this change came, I never wept for anyone. Compassion is where the truest power lies. Repeatedly, just before a healing or miracle is mentioned in the scriptures it says, "He [Christ] was moved to compassion" (Matthew 14:14, 15:32, 20:34). Furthermore, brokenness is not the enemy; in fact, it can bring substantial change of character to your life. Remember, adversity breeds champions.

In addition, something else has occurred as well. The stronghold of fear that has plagued me is withering away. Part of the process of walking through the passing of a loved one is various fears that hit hard at the same time. There's the fear of the emptiness, a future without them. What is the future going to be like with them absent? And your own mortality comes into view, just to name a few. The lostness I've felt has overwhelmed me at times. These, among many fears, are the "bricks" that build the stronghold of fear itself. The death of a loved one has the potential to expose the fears that were present all along but never really seen.

Shortly after my son's death, I was set free from what some call "the fear of man." Oh, yes, it's real all right, especially if you've suffered abuse from others. One of its many destructive functions is to cause a person to take an offense at every turn in relationships with others. There's an undercurrent emotionally on the inside that always anticipates being wronged by someone. That puts a person in a defensive position in most relationships.

All I know is that among the other incredible changes of thought and character that have transpired, the recognition of fear's hold in my life is being systematically exposed and cast aside. A new freedom from Christ is rising like never before. At times, even in my workplace, an overwhelming joy overtakes me as I do my daily routines. It is amazing to feel this supernatural joy right in the middle of the grief. Is that joy an everyday occurrence? No, it is not, but I will lay hold of it whenever I can. My peace runs very deep now. Let the passing of your loved ones produce in you a journey filled with the love of God, a greater trust in Him, and fearlessness!

Sincerely,
Marguerite L. Woodall

MANY WORLDS, ONE KINGDOM

I've been contemplating the words of Christ when He said, "For where your treasure is, there will your heart be also" (Matthew 6:21). What about the "worlds" we create in our hearts and minds that affect the way we think? We seek the so-called "treasures" of pleasure, reward, or self-importance in these worlds we mentally and emotionally create and participate in. Are what these worlds offering really the best treasures or rewards? What world are you choosing to live in daily?

If you live in the world of the fear of man, there is constant mistrust, and it distorts everything you hear and a constant emotional state of offense is your reward.

If you live in the world of worry or dread, you will try to control everything (or everyone around you) and be in a constant self-protective relational retreat in life. That takes a lot of energy.

If you live in the world of Cinderella, you will always be waiting for the handsome prince on a white horse to rescue you, when really, only one man as coming back on a white horse. His name as Faithful and True (Revelation 19:11).

If you live in the world of addiction, you are running from the pain that is meant to draw you to the God, who can comfort you and uses suffering in our fallen world to create a heart of compassion for others. Adversity breeds champions.

If you live in the world of the victim, nothing ever turns out the way you choose, and the glass is always half empty. It is the enemy of deep personal change in character.

If you live in the world of no absolutes, where there is no right or wrong; moral bankruptcy will be your companion. There will be no foundation called conviction, and integrity is sacrificed on the altar of self.

If you live in the world of Adonis or Narcissus, you're avoiding imperfection at all costs, and it becomes all about you. Then a beautiful transformation is missed that can take place in the person within through God's loving care and guidance.

If you live in the world of Cheers, "where everybody knows your name," then the friendships last only for the weekend, during the dark of night, or as long as you pursue a drunken life style. What then is the end result? You overlook the One who sticks closer than a brother, and frankly, I'd rather be called a "friend" of God.

If you live in the world of socialism, you're always a victim, and you want government or powerful men to be Robin Hood, taking from the rich to give to the poor when Christ Himself said, "*You* feed them."

If you live in the world of the Kingdom of God, forgiveness is its foundation. Love guards against any fear. Christ never fails you. Suffering produces endurance and compassion. You are an agent of change, not a victim. There is great peace in knowing what is right and what is wrong and following those convictions. It's not all about you, so relax. You are called the friend of God, and you know the buck stops with you.

—Marguerite Lever Woodall

GOD AND THE FAVORITE PHOTO

I just stared at the large cedar chest at the foot of my bed that day. Two years have passed now. My husband's grandfather had crafted two of the large chests for us when we were a young family. I was overwhelmed in those moments by a very stark realization. My husband and son are now gone, and there is no one left to pass the legacy of the chest's contents to. The tears came, and I cried out, "Oh, Father God! What do I do with all the memories in this cedar chest?" I wanted to pass them on to my son and hopefully a future family of his own. It struck me deeply that all those memories held no value for anyone other than myself now. What do you do with that?

The scrapbooks in that cedar chest were full of events and memories of my husband and me and our son. They almost overflowed out of it. Our travels, our marriage, my son's birth, and the years following as he grew into a young man were carefully and lovingly recorded in each one. Every year, I had put together a scrapbook of my son's life journey. There were photos of time spent with my folks and family members as well as my husband's over the years. Baby blankets, baby shoes, and every scrap of import had been stored there as only a mother can garner and keep about her kid—birthdays, school events, proms, and graduation memories included.

I had made sure to keep pictures of every event in his life until I had moved and he left home. Love does that; even all those random school homework papers were kept—you know, the ones with their very first attempts to draw pictures and letters in their first days of school. Several of my husband's things had also been set aside for my son at the time. He was four years old when his father died, and I had wanted him to know some part of his dad in the future in the carefully folded jackets and shirts, the wallet, the old aftershave, and the sunglasses among other things.

Some of the deepest pain came when I realized that no one would really, truly value them in the future. The photos and mementos let others know that we mattered in this life, that we had a life story. Then it struck me that the life stories of the love in those photos, the value I held for them, would mean nothing anymore to anyone. We all want to be remembered and, more importantly, valued, to be remembered with fondness and deepest love by those we leave behind when we die. I could imagine my son's sharing photos of me and his dad with his children in the future, saying, "This was my mom, your grandmother," or "This was my dad, your grandfather." There is no other son or daughter to pass them on to either, and other family members certainly couldn't care less about them. After all, I don't blame them; they have their own.

A part of the legacy that we physically leave behind is in those photographs and the trinkets we collect in the course of our lives. The contents of the cedar chests would not be passed down to my son now; he is gone. That realization was heartbreaking to me. The valuation of all those things would die with me. We are people who have lived, journeyed through life, and then are suddenly gone. Will anyone care?

I wanted, in those moments, for someone to care about this loss too. On the inside, I was screaming, "Will anyone remember that we were here? That our lives mattered? That we loved each other so much?" The cedar chest sits there, and I cannot open it and go through all those memories, not yet, not for some time. Indeed, I've wondered if I will ever be able to.

As I was writing this story, the Lord spoke and gently reminded me about a facet of our memories that we need to be aware of as well. We tend to build, at times, elaborate groupings of photographs for display in our homes. Memorabilia can abound around us and the various types of memorials of our loved ones too. Certainly, there is nothing wrong with remembering those we have loved and lost. However, we can become imprisoned by them if we're not careful.

I know of a youth who had died in a small town, and consequently, a statue and small memorials of him went up in several places city wide. Friends and family mourned with that mother when the boy passed after a long and brave battle with a devastating sickness. The memorials were from the townspeople's heart of compassion. They were a way for them to honor the boy's life and to express their heartfelt grief alongside his mother.

The memorials on one end of town and the opposite also is a constant reminder of this child's life and death when you drive by. As a result, I believe these reminders contributed to some degree the mother's not being able to let go of her child so that she could move on with her life. It's been ten years, and I see that perhaps too much memorializing of a loved one can become a trap, a trap of idolization of a person long gone.

The loved ones left behind cannot move forward because of it, and everyone else takes a back seat to the "memory" and memorializing of the deceased. It has tormented and wrecked many marriages when a child dies as the marriages take a back seat and becomes less of a priority as it should be. I don't want the memory of my son and husband to lock me away from a future with someone else if that comes. More importantly, I don't want it to distract me from my walk with God. I will grieve deeply for a time, knowing I am forever changed because they are gone, and then I must move on.

My son's closest friends were putting together a photo and video presentation of his life for the funeral service that Saturday. These friends had accumulated many pictures over the years of different adventures together they had had with Randall, many I had never seen. It was decided that family members speaking at the service would choose a favorite photo from the montage being created, and then a screen behind us would display it as we shared loving words of remembrance.

Here it was, the night before the funeral itself, and I only had a small handful of photos that I had brought with me on my flight from Oklahoma. I just grabbed something hastily in my state of shock. As I was randomly picking from the topmost part of the cedars chest's contents, I was not thinking about a video presentation. Truthfully, the pain of my son's death had numbed me to the point where I just didn't think about much beyond the moment. None of the photos presented in the upcoming montage stood out to me either.

Sitting at the table that evening with my sister Mary and my friend Brandi, I knew a decision had to be made about a photo that I wanted for the service. It meant the world to me to have just the right picture. I was at a loss, and I truly wanted a photo that represented my best and deepest love for my son and how much he meant to me. As I sat there, Mary spoke up and said, "What about your favorite photo? You know, the one of Randall standing in his crib when he was little?"

I was taken aback. How did she know that was my most beloved photo and memory of my son? I had never shared with her how much I loved that picture. "What do you mean?" I asked. She then told me about a visitation from God in a dream she had had the night before. He spoke to her directly and showed her my "favorite photo" that was in the cedar chest.

I had completely forgotten about it in my grief. Every mother has one picture that is held close to her heart above all others among a lifetime of photographs. That particular photo of my son was taken in the early morning when he was a small child. There he was, looking out over his crib, railing with his blue one-piece pajama suit on. I walked into his room to pick him up out of his crib as his little face was beaming with an angelic smile that greeted me, and his hair was standing on end!

It was too late. It was the night before the funeral, and I certainly could not fly home to retrieve it in time. What I did not know was that Mary had already acted on the word from God and His instruction in her dream. She had asked a friend to go to my home and look through the cedar chest. The favorite photo had been secured and sent via a cell phone text. There it was, a mother's favorite photo to display as I spoke about my son at his funeral that Saturday. I was at a loss for words, impacted greatly by what God had done ahead of time for me. He had spoken to and directed my sister on my behalf in a dream. Being in the midst of the grief, I struggled to remember even the little things, even that favorite photo, but God remembered it for me.

What kind of God is this who knows what your favorite photo is anyway? What God moves heaven and earth speaking directly to someone to make sure you have what is needed most at the right time and on the right day? What kind of God-love is this that knows about and anticipates the choice of a heart's desire ahead of time when you yourself don't know about your own future need? I will never forget this small-yet-incredible move of God on my behalf. Indeed, I hope I never stop being awed about this amazing facet of God's love. And the most wonderful thing of all, He had placed His valuation on my photos and memories by remembering them for me and brought my favorite photo of my son to me from 1,200 miles away.

The following day, that photo silently spoke volumes on that screen, at least for me. It was about a mother's love for a child now gone and God's loving fulfillment of an unknown and unanticipated need. God valued my cedar chest photos, and I could also see that God became my memory when mine had failed me.

Randall Lee Woodall

Sorrow's Altar

H ow do you continue to worship God daily and pray when grief prevails every day? What does it look like to press forward in relationship with God even when all you can bring before Him is a broken heart, broken dreams, and a voided future with a loved one As I've spent my devotional time with the Lord in my mornings, I cry a lot, and it's difficult to stay focused in prayer. His presence is there every day, touching my heart, but I cannot tell if I weep because His presence is so strong and loving or if it is the grief welling up again inside of me.

God will share images with us about things of import to Him or to show us where we are at emotionally or spiritually as His children. My devotionals are an important daily routine for me, and they can set the tone for the entirety of my day. It is that measure of time to just sit and talk to God, to listen to Him, and to pour out my heart as well. God showed me an image one morning of what the devotional time I set aside looks like in the midst of my grief. It was a scene of someone who was trying very hard to continue relationship with Him despite the frequent sorrow.

In the image, I saw myself approaching a large stone altar to worship and pray to God. The altar was in the middle of a small meadow. There were several items I was carrying in my arms to this place of worship. Indeed, there were so many items that I was close to spilling everything on the ground before I could reach it. I halfway spilled and also poured them out onto the surface of the altar as I fell against it. My items scattered and bounced across the top in disarray. Some were the tools of worship, others are gifts of thanks to God, some are small burdens and requests, and also one broken heart in desperate need of healing. At the same time, I also dropped to one knee on the ground with my head down and a single hand gripping the altar's edge as I break down and weep. But I must get up and move forward again.

I felt like a small child still trying to bring everything I could, everything I am or have, to God's altar to worship and spend time with Him no matter what. The feelings of a little kid with too much to carry in her arms and nearly dropping it all on the ground before reaching the table to put it down overwhelmed me. I felt so small.

For those of us who try to follow God despite the deepest grief, I believe this image speaks volumes. This is what I do know: I will continue to come before God daily in a time of worship and prayer. I cannot let grief stop or derail my relationship with Him. It would be easy to forget for a time or walk away in the midst of everything that has happened, and who could blame me? I believe He understands when I am distracted by the pain and grief at times. As I come to sit and talk to Him and share my heart, He still waits for me every day.

THE D-WORD

The Thanksgiving holiday has come once again. Since my son's death the year before, I hadn't realized in the midst of my grief at that time what a huge pall had been cast over the previous year's celebration for everyone around me. I guess I was legitimately oblivious or probably still in a state of shock. In retrospect, that shock mercifully lasted for some time. How did I make it through that particular Thanksgiving after burying my son one month before?

I have found that I've feared saying out loud that my son died. It's the word "died" that's disturbing to me. I don't fear the word *passed* or *gone* or any other word denoting an absence, just the word *died*. I'm sure I'm not alone in this. I wonder, is it the finality of the word itself? The phrase "cut off" comes to mind also (not in a judgmental way) as in being cut off from life here in this world. How brutal that sounds.

Is the revulsion, fear, and finality of this word that I feel because it's not natural for us as human beings to even know what death is or the word that describes it? Mankind was not originally designed to die. We were made by God to live forever. Death entered through Adam and Eve's declaration of independence from God. A very large part of us, perhaps it's in our DNA, still has the innate knowing that we were never designed by God to die. I believe that is why it impacts us so deeply and changes us. At the beginning of creation, it was not natural for us to experience termination of any kind, but now, it happens all the time.

We were meant to live life in its truest sense in immortality, and a part of us, deep down, knows it. Because of this, the word *death* or the event itself, we suspect was never meant to be.

I've thought a lot about what was never meant to be. Then God gently reminds me that there is more than one kind of death.

Never Meant to Be

The early death in youth,
Causes me to face my own mortality
Then I ask the question…
What was never meant to be?
The evil in men that stalks us all around
The constant shifting of men's hearts
Where is the solid ground?
None of this was meant to be.
I ponder this, what was never meant to be.
The deaths of those we love, the aging of life
And every tragedy.
Relationships shipwrecked by strife.
God seemingly distant from these;
This also was never meant to be.
All of this man's sin ushered in,
These things never meant to be.
We were never meant to face mortality.
All of this, and in man's heart it lingers still,
What was really meant to be
Our hearts cry out for Eden,
The remembrance of God's eternity.

—Marguerite Lever Woodall

(Ecclesiastes 3:11)

GOD AND THE TWO-STEP VICTORY

*R*egrets come when a loved one dies—you know, the "would have, could have, should have" mantra. It seems to be an automatic part of the process we go through when tragedy strikes. However, it can be dangerous spiritually. As a Christian, I also know that the enemy of our soul will take a tactical advantage against us with regrets if we dwell on them too long; it's names are Condemnation and Guilt. With this in mind, I choose to share a "regret" that haunted me for some time after my son's death. This is not something I share lightly, and it is deeply painful. My hope is that I'm surely not the only person on the planet who has gone through this particular regret. But first, let me share this.

My husband died suddenly when our son was four. I forced myself to walk up to the casket, to touch him, to kiss his forehead, to smooth his clothes one last time, and to say goodbye. Then my mother suddenly passed on Mother's Day a few years later. I again, forced myself to face death by going in to see her one last time before the cremation. I wanted to tell her I loved her and would miss her deeply. After smoothing the wrinkles on the sheet draped over her, I kissed her on the forehead in a final goodbye.

In the month of February, over a decade later, I held my dad's hand as he died in front of me. Despite his cruelty over the years, I loved my father, and I had decided that no one deserves to die alone. There was a promise I had made to myself that I would not let that happen to him. I was the only one there in the room with him when he died, and truthfully, I thought I'd lose my mind because of the pain and finality of the death I witnessed. To actually be present when death occurs is difficult.

What was my regret? It is this: that I could not walk up to the casket where my son's body had been placed to touch him, smooth his jacket, tell him I loved him, and give him a mother's kiss. For three days at the funeral home, as we were making the various arrangements, I tried to walk up to my son and could not. I could not move beyond the last row of pews up front. His casket was still fifteen feet away. There was only a partial view of his face from the distance where I stood. I could not walk up to him; I could not say goodbye. It was as though there was an invisible wall that was stopping me, and I could not move myself farther forward. I felt paralyzed. What was this? Why was I sensing this wall? Was my mind stopping me, or was it God. Did God know it would be more than I could bear, but I did not?

Perhaps all the sudden deaths I had been through held me back from my son's side. Was it the culmination of all the sudden-death events in my life that made me feel I could not take on one more, especially with it being my only child, my son? The loss of a child is the worst death to endure of all. On the last day just before the funeral service itself, I mustered all the courage I could within myself and took two more steps beyond that last row of pews that I had not been able to take before. It was then that I could more fully see my son's face despite the distance that still remained. But I was still at least ten feet away instead of fifteen.

Moments later, I shared my struggle with the hospice pastor and told him about the two extra steps I was able to take. "But I could not take more than those two steps," I said as I wept.

He replied, "Marguerite, don't you see? That was your two-step victory!"

Those kind words helped me for a time, and they pulled me through the rest of the day's events. However, I was still carrying the guilt and grief at the same time for not walking up to the casket and to my son. I was afraid of seeing my son's face in death.

Several months later, I shared my struggle with the guilt and condemnation of this event, and my pastor and friends began praying for me. Two days later, as I sat in a time of prayer myself, I sensed God was impressing me with a special truth, and I knew my friends' prayers were impacting me. The truth is this: I *will* have the final and greatest victory. It will be a three-step victory, not two. The third step I take will be the one final and greatest step of all. It will be an eternal victory. What is this triumph? When I also pass from this world and walk up to my son again, and he will greet me. I will walk up to him without a casket between us, touch him, hold his face and kiss it, smooth the robe he's wearing, and say hello, not goodbye.

CHOOSE LIFE

This is a subject most run away from in a conversation, much less let anyone know it has assaulted them emotionally at some point in their lives. What do I speak of? Suicide. I never expected to write on this subject. But here I am tackling it anyway. The immediate thinking would be that this has not touched you personally in any way. However, you may find yourself needing to choose life where you did not know you hadn't to begin with or help a close friend to choose life who has given up on it. My hope is that this will, at the very least, give you insight to reach out to others meaningfully who struggle with living sometimes.

As I walked by my refrigerator one day, I looked at a recent photo of my son I had placed there. It had been a year and a half since he had passed from the accidental drug overdose, and I'd only just begun to grieve my loss. He was my only child. As I stood there, I was suddenly and unexpectedly overwhelmed by a sudden suicidal emotion. It swept over and engulfed me like a tidal wave. Visually, in my mind's eye, I saw it, a large deep black hole of pain that looked like it had no bottom. I knew instinctively not to allow it to swallow me. Frankly, it took me by surprise. It passed as quickly as it came when I chose to stand against it as a follower of Christ and because my trust in God sustained me in those moments. The God that I know cares deeply for me.

It's hard to share this knowing that others may "label" me because of it. However, to me, it's worth it because it exposes another potential contributing factor in suicide and reveals our deep need for Christ's healing when we lose someone we love.

Years ago, I stood in front of a man, asking him a question. He had just finished his most recent talk for the evening. As a guest speaker at a local church that night, this man was known as "Mr. Agape" in Christian circles nationwide. His nickname was "the Apostle of Love." His reputation as a Christlike, loving man was widely known. He spoke extensively on laying aside old practices and habits in our lives that cause harm or discredit us as followers of Christ or hinder our walk with God. I asked him what thoughts he might have as to why quitting smoking in my life was so very difficult and seemed impossible to stop. The addiction had an iron grip on me. He was silent for some time (which I know that he was listening to the Holy Spirit in those moments), then tears welled up in his eyes, and he said, "Some people choose a slow form of suicide, not an immediate one."

That statement opened the door to the understanding that embedded within an addiction, there can possibly be a form of slow suicide occurring, and we don't "see" it for what it is. Somewhere in our life journey, a hidden part of us on the inside can make a decision that life is not worth living, that we are not valued, and we have no purpose or direction. There can be a multitude of abusive life events that bring us to this internal decision: a parent's absence or abandonment, physical or emotional abuse itself, or any kind of perceived rejection from others in our life to name only a few. As a result, we come to a place where we reject ourselves and begin to punish ourselves through the addictions. The feeling or belief that we were not supposed to even be here to participate in life is at play, and it is not a conscious realization most often. It is a strange atonement for perceived guilt.

Of course, the methods of slow suicide are varied and numerous, and truly, no condemnation on my part as meant here—been there, done that. There's a multitude of different kinds of addictions, including man-made narcotics or nature's natural chemicals found in the environment. The addictions can manifest as well in our appetites with excessive food consumption. Another often overlooked one is a "flirting" with death through extreme sport activities that greatly lessen each time one's odds of living through another "adventure." I call it the "adrenaline addiction." One becomes addicted to the need for more of their own adrenaline being produced in "daredevil" situations.

The other end of the spectrum on this issue is the more immediate suicidal actions people take that can stem from deep emotional pain. The emotional agony that we are exposed to through life events can run very deep and feel very overwhelming. The pain, at times, feels so strong that it seems like the only "escape" from it is ending one's life as quickly as possible. The fear generated by it is off the chart. In those moments, self-medicating is not working either. The powerlessness we feel threatens to undo us. Deep emotional pain feels and looks like death. God has been teaching me through the years to not fear it. He is there if we reach out to Him in those moments. Our problem is that we demand relief from our pain in any way we can without Him.

Can demonic spirits be involved in suicidal issues? Yes. My focus, however, is not on what the enemy tries to do but rather what leaves us vulnerable to the attack to begin with. We deeply need Christ's healing touch emotionally in many areas of our lives.

I do not know if this will ever confront you in your life or not. I think it does more than others are willing to admit. For those of you who grieve like myself, I pray you will lean on the God who loves us all and can see you through it. Know this: you're not alone, and this is nothing new to life's struggles. I have chosen life and will continue to do so.

The greatest victory I can have here is to live to fight another day. I want to be used by God to make the devil pay for his duplicity in trying to get us to abort our lives before the time. Unfortunately, he succeeded with my son through addiction. My vengeance is to fulfill every good work that God has purposed for me in my life journey before I pass. My payback is to love with Christ's love and to live. Check yourself through God's leading and don't allow suicide of any kind to rule you. I know the One that vanquished suicide. He cares. He can heal and deliver. And by the way, I did defeat that forty-five-year-old nicotine habit that was slowly killing me. Christ set me free when I chose life—His.

GOD AND THE TIME CLOCK REDEMPTION

Return and say to Hezekiah the leader of My people, "Thus says the Lord, the God of your father David, I have heard your prayer, I have seen your tears; behold, I will heal you. On the third day you shall go up to the house of the Lord." (2 Kings 20:5)

And Isaiah said, "This shall be the sign to you from the Lord, that the Lord will do the thing that He has spoken: shall the shadow go forward tens steps or go back ten steps?"
So King Hezekiah answered, "It as easy for the shadow to decline ten steps; no, but let the shadow turn backward ten steps."
And Isaiah the prophet cried to the Lord, and He [God] brought the shadow on the stairway back ten steps by which it had gone down on the stairway of Ahaz. (2 Kings 20:9–11)

In Old Testament times, when a king's palace was built, there was a time piece typically added to the structure during its construction. Often, it would have been a strategically placed set of palace stairs attached to the outside of the structure. The stairs themselves became a sundial of its own where the sun's path could be tracked during the day. One was able to tell the advancing time of day by observing how far the sun's shadow had moved forward from the top of the staircase down it's steps. King Hezekiah was asking God to briefly reverse the time of day, as a sign that he would be healed, by having the advancing shadow on the palace stairs go backward up toward the top where it had started that morning.

I think of all the movies that have been made about going back in time, reversing it, or indeed going forward in time too. Man has dreamed of manipulating time for centuries. How awesome it is that God would reverse a portion of time during a particular day to reassure this king of his promised healing.

Along those lines of thought, I'm also reminded of the biblical term called "redemption." By definition, to redeem something means, in a general sense, to buy back something or to bring about deliverance as a result of a transaction. Then there's the redeeming of time or "buying up an opportunity" where time is a season. I think of redemption also in the sense of being rescued, a reversal or deliverance out of bad circumstances or delivered out of a situation just in the nick of time. This is a story of the literal redemption of time in my life or reversal, a "buyback" if you will, and the healing that was given when it was needed most.

Knowing that I've needed healing and change in my life on a personal level, part of my journey has been learning about ministries that teach it. I had witnessed at this point many memories of abuse and trauma healed by Christ through a prayer ministry called Theophostic (Greek for "God's light"). Some years ago, a close friend and I were learning together how to be more focused in the leading of God's Spirit when praying for others through this unique prayer ministry. We met together periodically to pray for each other too. As I sat down with my friend on this particular night in my home, it was with reluctance as I had been significantly ill for several days. The exhaustion I had been experiencing had taken its toll on me, and I had almost canceled our meeting that evening.

The week previously had been tough. Suddenly, within just a few days' time, I had gained a significant amount of weight, a total of three pant sizes' worth! I'd been forced to purchase new pants for my work attire. What I had no longer fit me. My lungs became congested and filled with fluid. Breathing had become difficult as well.

Mentally, while at work, I felt like I was walking through a fog. On top of that, fatigue was plaguing me daily. As I left work on one of those evenings that week, I came close to blacking out as I walked out the door to go home, and it frightened me. The possibility that I was suffering from a severe case of pneumonia had entered my mind, but I had decided to see a physician at a later date when I felt I could get away from my work.

As we prayed together sitting at my kitchen counter and invited God to speak to us for His leading and healing where it was needed, an image came clearly to my mind, and I knew God's presence was moving. I saw myself running up the side of a large mountain with the goal of laying my heart on a stone altar dedicated to God at the summit. I ran to the top of the summit at what seemed like a supernatural speed, and it was with a sense of urgency that I also felt at the same time.

The understanding came to me that I had been holding back a part of my heart from the Lord in my life. My heart had been crushed as a child through abuse and rejection. I had learned not to share my heart with others for the fear of being rejected. As a result, my heart became hardened and very cold. In those moments, as I sat there, I knew that I needed to give all of my heart on that mountain's altar to the living God and to forsake the hardening of my heart as well. Simultaneously, I remembered being perplexed by the supernatural speed and urgency with which I saw myself going up the mountain side in that image.

What happened next was unlike anything I've ever experienced before. I can only describe it as a massive lifting sensation of an incredibly huge heavy weight that was on top of me that I had been oblivious to. The "lifting" I felt coming off of my head and my shoulders area flowed from me like a mighty massive river and seemed to travel upward through the roof of my home directly above me.

As the impact of what I was physically feeling was happening, my friend suddenly sat backward abruptly in her chair with a look of amazement on her face. She said, "I'm seeing a vision of a clock. The clock is large, and its hands are spinning backward. The hands are spinning backward and increasing in speed as they do so."

Immediately after she had voiced what she was seeing, she began gripping her left arm in evident pain. "My left arm is hurting me horribly, as though I'm having a heart attack, but I know I am not having one."

Neither of us were sure about what was happening in those moments. God had been moving incredibly, no doubt, but what did it all mean? Why was He giving a vision of a clock with hands spinning backward in time? Why was my friend physically "feeling" the symptoms of a heart attack when she in fact wasn't having one? What was the massive lifting sensation that I was experiencing? Everything came to a halt shortly afterward as the movement and direction of God's Spirit gently ceased thirty minutes later. My friend and I said our goodbyes as she left for the evening. Being somewhat perplexed by the night's events and exhausted from the physical illness I had been battling, I retired for the night.

The following morning, as I stood in my kitchen with my cup of coffee in hand, I began to slowly realize that something was vastly different. The thought came to my mind that my heart felt like the heart of a seventeen-year-old! In my midforties at the time, my heart felt light, young, and strong again. It was then, in those following moments, that I realized that there was no fluid buildup in my body anymore. In fact, it was gone. It had disappeared overnight. My lungs were no longer drowning in liquid; they were clear, as though I had never been sick at all. As I stood there, it hit me like a freight train. I had gone to bed the night before feeling very ill and wondering if I should go to an emergency room and woke up the next morning completely healed.

A quiet, gentle "voice" spoke to me that I have come to know as God's, and He said, "Look up the symptoms of heart failure." Still dressed in my pajamas, I immediately began to research about heart failure via my computer. Congested lungs and shortness of breath—yes. Rapid fluid and water retention resulting in abdominal and ankle swelling and sudden weight gain—yes. Dizziness, weakness, and fatigue—yes. Rapid or irregular heartbeats—yes. It was then that I realized that God had healed me of heart failure in its final stages the night before. The knowing also came that had I not been healed that evening before, I would not have made it through to the next morning.

For many years, I had a heart condition that plagued me physically, the condition known as PAT, or paroxysmal atrial tachycardia, as a sudden rapid heart rate that can be difficult to stop when it is triggered. It was brought under control with the prescription medication Lanoxin. As a by-product of the foxglove plant, it is actually a poison used in low dosage amounts to control rapid heart rate conditions such as PAT. I was eventually switched to another medication for the problem after several years and had a surgery later to correct the condition permanently. However, I am firmly convinced that the Lanoxin was also slowly killing my heart physically from its long-term use.

As I marveled at my healing in those moments and was comprehending what had happened to me, the revelation came that the vision of the clock with its hands spinning backward faster and faster represented the reversal or redemption of time from the premature aging of my heart that had brought me into heart failure. The Lord had redeemed the time for my heart physically, and the aging had been reversed by several years. That was why my heart felt so young, so vibrant, and not weighted down as it had been for so long!

The realization also came that an impending heart attack had been taken away as well. The symptoms of a heart attack that my friend had felt physically that was not hers foreshadowed an imminent heart attack that I was going to have. God had stopped it before it could come to pass. This was why my race to the top of the mountain in the image God showed me was so supernaturally swift. It had to be. I was dying that night and did not know it. It began to slowly dawn on me that what I had experienced and my friend had witnessed was a lifesaving miracle, and we did not understand it when it transpired. I called her and excitedly shared with her about my healed heart and body and my thoughts on what had happened. She was as much in shock as I was as we both began to realize the magnitude of God's great grace in saving my life when I didn't even realize it was in such grave danger.

After getting dressed that morning, I ran outside. I ran all over the place! I was running the full length of my country property, up two flights of stairs, and back down. For the first time in many, many years, I was not out of breath. My heart did indeed feel like that of a seventeen-year-old! As I tried to grasp the magnitude of the miraculous healing I was given, I exclaimed to God, "Lord, You reversed the aging of my heart! You healed me of heart failure and took away an impending heart attack!" Then I asked Him, "But where in the Bible does it talk about You reversing time for someone like this?"

Then I heard God's whispered reply, and He said, "It was also Hezekiah's story."

THE TRAVELERS

The two travelers had been walking some distance in the heavy desert sands. They stopped and stood in front of what looked like a small hut, a resting place in the middle of the seemingly endless sea of sand. The sun had gone down long ago. The Man, standing to the left of the woman, held her with His right hand and arm wrapped around her shoulders to hold her up. You could see the fatigued slump of her body as she had become worn and tired from the journey to this point. The Man lifted the torch in His left hand higher in the darkness of the night to find the entry into the desert hut, which was a place of rest for a time. The light from the torch illuminated His shoulder-length dark hair, white robe, and sandals.

The woman looked down at the sand all around the hut as the torchlight revealed that it had been trampled heavily and was not smooth as windswept desert sand would usually be. *Deserts were not often traveled*, she thought, *so the sand should be smooth or exhibit a windswept pattern instead.* This sandy area had been well traveled and was full of footprints, many of them. Others had been this way before.

ANOTHER COUNTRY

As I sat and prayed in the early morning hours and listened for God's voice, I also reflected on an upcoming trip to Europe. I had planned the trip for three years for my son and I. Randall was excited as I shared with him some of the events planned for it. As each of those three years passed, I steadily put every bit of extra income that I could toward it. We would stay in Rome for a week, then board a ship for a seven-day cruise of the Mediterranean, visiting different ports of call in Italy, Spain, and France. This would be a grand adventure for both of us. I wanted to connect more deeply with my son during the trip.

I had stayed in Florida for fifteen years after my husband's death instead of moving to the West Coast and living by my own family. It was important to me for Randall to finish high school and to spend time with his grandparents and friends instead of uprooting him. After those years had passed, the Lord placed it upon my heart to move to another state to be with family that I had not come to know more because of an early move in my youth.

Though I wanted my son to move with me, he chose to stay. That left us both with monthly phone calls and only an occasional visit from each other out of state when our finances permitted. It was very heart-wrenching at times for me being apart from my son and just wanting to be present to hold him when he was down or needed me or to celebrate a life event with him. For me, this trip would also be a time of reconnection and hopefully a deeper one between my son and I since my move.

My reflections this particular morning were of the ruins of Rome and what it would have been like for Randall to have seen all of the majesty that was once a civilization to be reckoned with. I have a deep love and passion for ancient civilizations, the ruins that are left behind, and how those peoples lived in their times historically. The Roman Forum, Palatine Hill, the Colosseum, and Pompeii had been on the itinerary for us.

Not quite two years after Randall's death and having put the trip off more than once because of it, I decided to go forward with the plans. The expenses had been paid for ahead of time, and there would be significant financial loss if I did not go. I shared with the Lord about the deep sadness in my heart that my son would not be going on the trip I had planned for us for so long. I lamented out loud and offhandedly said, "Lord, Randall will not be with me to see the magnificent ancient ruins from long ago that I so much wanted him to see."

When I arose moments later as my devotional time came to a close and I began to walk away, I heard God distinctly and plainly say, "Your son is seeing a far greater country, without the ruins of men."

Instead, they were longing for a better country—a heavenly one. Therefore, God is not ashamed to be called their God, for He has prepared a city for them.

—Hebrews 11:6

God, Delta Air Lines, and Both Escorts

It was 10:30 a.m. when I arrived at the Mobile, Alabama, airport, and I was headed back to Tulsa, Oklahoma. My son had been laid to rest, and I had to return home. My sister Mary had already flown home the day before. The airport car rental needed to be turned back in by 11:00 a.m. Unfortunately, my flight would not depart until 5:30 p.m. that evening. I hadn't realized that when I made the flight reservation that the car rental return policy would leave me sitting in the airport for six hours before my flight home. How was I going to bear walking around the airport, grief-stricken, for the next six hours? It felt like more than I could emotionally handle. It was a difficult, scary fifty-mile drive to the airport that morning too. I felt so lost, and I was hurting so much. The feeling that I just couldn't take any more stressful emotional situations for a while threatened to overtake me. Even trying to do simple or normal things were hard. I was alone.

In the terminal waiting area, I approached Delta's gate desk to speak to an airline agent. "Are there any possible openings on a flight to Tulsa earlier today than the 5:30 p.m. one tonight?" I asked.

"No," she said. Then as a side thought, she voiced a complaint out loud, which baffled me, and she added, "The pilot for the eleven-o'clock flight this morning is mysteriously late. He's disappeared, and we can't locate him."

I remembered wondering what on earth that comment had to do with my question or my situation.

I headed toward the airline's ticket counter shortly after with the hope that if I was put on standby, there would be an earlier flight I could take if someone else did not show. The $50 fee placed on my charge card for it was worth it to me if I could fly home more quickly. With a brief prayer under my breath, as I walked away, I said, "Lord, I am so tired. I'm grieving so much for my son. I'll be crying here all day with everyone looking at me, and I feel so lost. I cannot bear sitting here for the next six hours. Instead of leaving here at five thirty this evening, would You bring me home to Tulsa by then?"

As I sat in the airport cafeteria for an early lunch, I thought about the arrangements made at the funeral home a few days before. The question of the availability of a police escort for the hearse and funeral procession to the cemetery after the funeral services was discussed. We were told there would be no escort. There were too many funerals in the area that weekend, and no police officers were available for my son's funeral. The funeral director, to his credit, had called twice and was turned down both times.

The lack of a traditional police escort was hurtful. It is one last gesture of honor for the deceased and their family as they drive to the local cemetery and final resting place. With His divine interventions on our behalf throughout the entire week, God had made me feel like I was a daughter of a King and Randall, one of His beloved sons, a son of the King. Every detail came together supernaturally, and not one need was left unmet. I remembered thinking that God would handle things His way, and no escort was okay. If God wanted us to have one I thought, He would make a way.

As the funeral service concluded that Saturday afternoon and everyone was waiting to be dismissed, the funeral director walked up to the front of the chapel and made an unexpected announcement. His voice boomed out loudly in front of the gathered crowd across the chapel room as he spoke. He said, "Mrs. Woodall, I don't know what friends you have in high places, but you now have your funeral escort."

Indeed, I do have a Friend in high places, I thought (as my mouth hung open in amazement one more time).

A little-known family friend who had worked for a local sheriff's department had called in a favor unbeknownst to me. I was informed later that it was a retired sheriff's organization, who volunteer as funeral escorts, and it was stressed to me that they escorted VIPs and dignitaries only.

As I reflected on this memory at the sandwich bar, a Delta Air Line representative approached my table thirty minutes later. I was handed airline passes to Tulsa with an arrival time of five thirty that evening. It was the rescheduled morning flight of the pilot, who had been mysteriously late and could not be found. I had a second escort home, and this time, it was just for me. Unlike the pilot who was eventually found half an hour late for this flight, something else never was: the charge on my credit card for the standby fee.

My Father loves His daughter and her son, and I am humbled that He honored me.

THE THREE IMAGES OF GRIEF

O ver a series of months, as I've sat quietly in a daily time of prayer, Christ has reached out to me in a special way. At times, I have found that He will speak to me in a picture language or image to communicate His love and comfort for me when it is needed most. Not all may "hear" God this way, although I believe everyone can be touched by God in this manner if He so chooses. Three times now, as I've quietly listened for God's direction in this time of prayer, He has shown me different images each time.

The highway of holiness is not a wide road. I sat down on the side of this road on my journey to Zion to grieve again. I noticed the crushed white rock it was composed of. My multicolored, wide-striped robe with the belt at my waist was a darker color compared to the Man who walked up to me in His. His was a rough-woven white one. He was chewing on the end of a piece of grass like we do as kids growing up. He had a thoughtful smile on His face as He approached me. Then He sat down next to me, saying nothing. My silent tears streaming down my dusty face looked like trails. We both sat there in silence in our very Jewish-looking robes, with no words spoken and watching others pass by. Then He quietly put His arm around my shoulder and left it there. He sits with me.

The dust of mourning was flying high into the air as I knelt on the ground, bent completely forward. I was grabbing handfuls of the dust, throwing it over myself, and weeping just as it was for the Middle Eastern custom for mourning. My hair and head were so caked with dust that I looked like a clay figure with tears running down my face. I noticed then that someone else was kneeling beside me doing the same. He was throwing the dust as I did and was weeping and wailing loudly with me also. As I turned my head to look at

Him, I could see that His head and face was just as coated with caked on dust as mine! A small inner smile hit me emotionally then when I looked at us both. His hand reached out to touch my shoulder, and He quietly said, "There is hope for a better day." He mourns with me.

The funeral procession walk down the chapel isle was not easy. My bottom lip quivered as I tried to maintain control over a very loud lament that wanted to rush forward from my lips. The chapel's usher had taken my hand and placed it in the crook of his arm to walk me out of the funeral home after the service was done. The Lord brought this memory to me today. When I looked at it again, He was there instead. Dressed in His rough-woven white robe, with my hand in the crook of His arm, we walked down the aisle together as the service ended. His hand was gently placed over the top of my own. He walked out with me.

THE SANBALLAT FACTOR

During a time of morning devotionals, I thought about a recent decision that I had made. I would not lose one more night's sleep over someone taking an offense that was not intended by me or imagined by them. Have you known those who are so hurt and abused by life that it's difficult to relate to them or do life with them without some emotional upset occurring? I speak of the people in our relational sphere of life, work, or in family who make you feel like you need to walk on "eggshells" most of the time. Their perceived offenses hold everyone hostage emotionally, and no one knows what will happen next. Do you find yourself easily offended?

As I contemplated these things, an image from of the book of Nehemiah came to mind out of the Old Testament in the Bible. The statement I "heard" in my spirit was this: "Nehemiah was sent by the king to restore Zion [Jerusalem], to assess the damage to the walls and boundaries, and to then rebuild and restore the city." In those same moments, scenes or images of this historical event played out before me as I thought about what I had just heard. God was giving an overview of a portion of the story of Nehemiah and one of its applications to our lives in the present. At the same time, He quietly spoke within my heart and told me that people who are offended easily are listening to a Sanballat in their lives. "Who was Sanballat?" you might ask. This individual was a part of Nehemiah's story.

Nehemiah was a Jewish exile and slave who had become a cup-bearer to the king of Persia (Artaxerxes) in ancient times. He had requested of Artaxerxes to be allowed to return to his homeland to rebuild his nation's capital. The king graciously agreed and indeed even gave financial backing and funding for the mission as well as giving back the Jewish temple artifacts of worship. Those artifacts had been taken years beforehand when the city was ransacked.

This ancient city of Jerusalem, also known as Zion, had once thrived with community, relationships, commerce, and the worship of God. Due to continued disobedience to God by the Jewish people, enemies were sent against it to conquer it and tear it down. It's homes, businesses, and synagogues were destroyed or damaged. The gates, walls, and boundaries had been torn down, burned, or partially breached in different places. The city's enemies had done their best to bring as much destruction as possible.

With his arrival in Zion (Jerusalem), Nehemiah, after assessing the damage, began the work of rebuilding. It was not without opposition, however. Three men continuously harassed Nehemiah and the people who were attempting to rebuild it. They did not want to see the city live and thrive again. One man in particular who headed up the verbal, emotional, and psychological attacks to hinder the restoration was a man named Sanballat (a governor of Samaria). He mocked, threatened, tried to intimidate, and attempted trickery to stop the restoration of Zion by the Jewish people. At one point, he feigned an offer of friendship so he could assassinate Nehemiah. He baited Nehemiah in every way in an effort to thwart his mission.

In my spirit, I saw this man and his cohorts standing outside the walls of Zion shouting threats and lies while circling the city's broken-down outer boundaries as described in the scripture. At one point, the builders had to carry weapons as they worked to defend against any possible attacks by Sanballat and his cohorts. Sanballat pulled out every stop in order to derail Nehemiah's mission. The repair and restoration of Zion threatened it's enemies tremendously.

As I looked at this story, an understanding came from God's Spirit that this man Nehemiah was a "type" of Christ. The King, God, sends Christ's spirit to come into our lives when we ask Him to enter our hearts. Salvation comes when we recognize that the city of our souls is broken and breached by sin and that He (Christ) Himself comes to bring restoration to the city of Zion in our hearts that fell when Adam did. Indeed, the King gave Christ every gift of the Holy Spirit needed for us to rebuild and has everything needed to heal the breaches and destruction in our soul and spirit that come from the abuses life presents and to, more importantly, restore worship and relationship with the living God. Christ stands with us and will guard us against the enemy as we allow Him to "rebuild" and restore or heal those areas that need it most in our hearts.

The Lord was revealing to me how the enemy (Satan or sin) can taunt, goad, or threaten us through our thoughts just as Sanballat did standing outside the walls of Zion to stop it's restoration. The Sanballat in our life will circle the walls of the city of our soul or mind, speaking lies to try to stop the work of needed changes in our lives that Christ wants to bring. Most often, those lies cause us to take up offenses with others or to sin in some manner relationally or otherwise. Inflammatory thoughts that are allowed to run rampant in the mind can build offenses in our hearts and bring divisions. It's those fiery thoughts that come from nowhere (also known as self-talk) about how you will say this or do that if someone hurts you or might cause problems. What offenses have I taken with others because I listened to a Sanballat who whispered things against them that were not so or distorted my perspective and incited me to anger or unforgiveness?

There are also the thoughts of fear that overwhelm us too that a Sanballat will try to use to cripple trusting God in any given life situation as well. He will circle the city of Zion in the mind of our heart and will speak lies that are meant to divert, distract, accuse, cause fear (intimidate), or set us against one another as Jesus is moving to heal, change, restore, and rebuild the city of God in our hearts. What fear keeps creeping in to shut me down that stops Christ's redemptive and restorative work in me? And what about the thoughts of condemnation and shame that can be directed at us? Sanballat uses those "shout-outs" all the time to tear us down.

What about the distractions that occur during a church service? Is a Sanballat circling the city of Zion in my heart with his lies of distraction to pull me away from entering into worship by thinking about lunch or what someone may have said to hurt me last Sunday? I have to ask myself what distractions are going on in my thought life that are diverting me away from deeper intimacy with God.

I think the worst of Sanballat's accusatory words come with the loss of a loved one. Every regret is thrown at us. All the "I could have...," "I should have...," "Why didn't I...," or worse yet, "It's all my fault" and "I can't go on without them" come into play at some point. Sanballat will circle the walls of the Zion in your heart where it is broken by the death of your loved one and accuse you of many shortcomings in regard to your interaction and relationship with the person who has passed. This is some of the most devastating and insidious of all the enemy's accusations and shout-outs that can come during the grieving we go through. It will happen when Christ works to bring healing to our brokenness and restore our lives again beyond the grief.

Nehemiah thwarted Sanballat at every turn because he listened to God's leading and followed God's instructions. Let us allow Christ to do the rebuilding and restoration of the city of Zion in our hearts. I believe Christ is meant to be the wall, the gate, and gatekeeper for the protection of our lives as a citizen of Zion. Christ brings protection and victory in this life from the Sanballats that seek to destroy us if we will listen to Him and trust Him. Most of us make the fatal error of building our own walls to keep harm away. They are the walls of offense.

Zion's walls and gates keep the enemy out. However, the gates do have purpose. They are meant to be opened for relationships and the interactions that are led by God's Spirit and not to be opened to let in the enemy through lies and deception. Inside the city of Zion, there is meant to be righteous commerce and business and thriving relationships. We should not be afraid to open those gates as Christ leads. His love guards those gates very well when they are open for relational interaction and daily commerce. We are not threatened by the enemy's taunts and accusations nor are we to be distracted by them as we focus on the goal, the prize of the high calling: to love and live well.

In the book of Isaiah 61:1–3, it refers to Christ coming into our lives to bring gladness, healing, freedom, and restoration. He wants to establish the kingdom of God and the Zion of the heart in us. But it also goes on to speak of you and I becoming "repairers of the breaches" (the brokenness caused by abuse) in others' lives through the love of Christ in us. For that reason, I will not live in the fear of offense or offending someone, but rather, I will live in the sphere of the love of God that supersedes it. I've also purposed to be aware when the enemy is taunting or baiting me to take up offenses. Christ will be the gatekeeper of my heart, the strong tower of my defense, the restorer of the breaches in my life, and the chief cornerstone of the city of Zion in my heart.

So what does Sanballat shout out about or say to you in your thought life to distract you? Who will control your thoughts? Will it be you and Christ in you or Sanballat and his cohorts with his accusations and taunts as they circle the walls of your city Zion? I researched and looked up the meaning of the name Sanballat. Names can have very significant meaning, especially Jewish ones. It means "the god sin has given life." I urge you, don't let Satan's (Sanballat's) lies and accusations *give birth to sin* in yours.

Great is the peace of those who love Thy law, and
nothing shall by any means offend them.

—Psalm 119:165

GOD AND THE LIAR

I stood in the doorway of my home, listening on the phone as the physician spoke. It was cancer. I was leaving to attend my first grief support group meeting that evening when I received the doctor's call. I can't begin to describe the feelings of lostness, pain, and fear that I was experiencing in those moments. It felt like the "other shoe" had finally dropped. Still in the midst of grieving over the loss of my son a year and a half earlier, I wondered how was I going to cope with this and all it entails emotionally, mentally, and physically at the same time. The voice of fear began to whisper to me, bringing to my mind every imaginable scenario involving impending doom and death from the diagnosis just given.

There is a stronghold of fear in my life, and it has plagued me on many fronts for many years. Fear is multifaceted. There's the fear of death, fear of lack in our finances, fear for a loved one's safety, fear of the unknown, and the list goes on and on. And those fears rise at various times to try and consume us like a wildfire if it can.

I shared the cancer diagnosis with one of my closest friends in a phone call as I walked across the church parking lot that night to attend the grief share meeting. In the following minutes of our phone conversation, God stepped into my moments of pain and fear. My friend began to share about an image spiritually she was seeing from the Lord simultaneously at the same time. She described a bonfire and a spirit of fear was dancing around it, throwing its lies into the fire as fuel to cause it to flare up and grow larger and spread. It was trying to shift my focus mentally and emotionally with its lies of fear to try to consume me. She was being shown the battle in my mind as the enemy was trying to convince me that I would die from the cancer.

Then in the midst of the conversation, the movement of God's Spirit and His voice came through suddenly, boldly, and with unmistakable clarity. God said, "Whose report will you believe?"

I was taken aback, and I wasn't sure if He was speaking about the diagnosis itself being in error or that the cancer meant my imminent death. I replied and asked God, "Which report do You mean, Lord?"

The Lord said, "The report from the enemy that this means your death or My report that it does not—whose report will you believe?"

God's presence permeated the atmosphere all around me in the parking lot when He spoke. As I stood there; the fear of Lord hit me like a ton of bricks. He was demanding an answer. I quickly replied out loud, "I will believe the report of the Lord."

Those words were hardly past my lips when God revealed to me an interpretation or understanding about a part of the vision I saw the day my son died a year and a half earlier that I had not understood before. It had baffled me for some time. I remembered seeing in the vision three bonfires on a remote island's beach that the enemy (local islanders or pirates historically) had lit to lure unsuspecting ships seeking safe harbor as storms at sea approached. Hidden reefs underwater in the harbor tore the ships apart instead. The result was shipwreck and the ship's cargo floating ashore for the island's natives or pirates for plunder.

I had also seen a tall red-and-white-striped lighthouse in the vision situated on a large solid rock outcropping of land farther down the shoreline. I knew it was the true light of guidance for the ships that approached and could be trusted to guide them to the safest harbor (which represented Christ). It was the number of bonfires on the first beach in the vision that was a mystery to me for some time, and I had wondered often why there was three of them on the island's shore instead of one. It was in those moments as I stood in the church parking lot that I received the interpretation of what those three bonfires represented.

The first bonfire represented the death of my husband in 1988. His death was meant to "shipwreck" a deeper commitment I had made in my life toward God, to cause me to question God's goodness. The second bonfire represented the death of my son Randall. This also was meant to "shipwreck" my faith and my trust in God with regard to my son's salvation. I momentarily assumed the third bonfire was representative of my death, but God's Spirit corrected me quickly. It was the fear of death that I needed to face and overcome by trusting God as I have never trusted Him before. The spirit of fear was trying to "shipwreck" my faith in God to keep me by stoking the flames of the third bonfire with the lies of imminent physical destruction and death from the cancer diagnosis. God had stepped into those moments to speak and rebut the lies the fear was trying to prompt me to accept.

I was emotionally exhausted when I went home that night. Sleep was a welcome relief from a tumultuous day to say the least. Not only did I share about my son's passing at the grief share meeting, but I also shared about the cancer diagnosis I'd received only an hour before my arrival. As I slept that night, I kept hearing someone singing a song to me. *Whose voice is that?* I thought. The mysterious voice sang it over and over again to me into the early morning hours. The song was "Fear Is a Liar." Why was this "voice" emphasizing this song as I slept? This was not a mental recollection from listening to the radio. It was a literal "voice" of some sort that was singing it to me into the night.

I instinctively knew God was trying to communicate something. The next morning, as soon as I could, I quickly searched the Internet on my computer for this song. There was an urgency in my spirit as I did so. The song writer was Zack Williams. I was only interested in the lyrics, not the video, I told myself. What were the words in that song? I remembered vaguely hearing it on the radio a couple times but did not pay attention closely to all the words. It must be important for me to know the lyrics, I thought to myself.

The official music video on YouTube that I found showed several life scenes that expressed the message of the song's lyrics as most music videos do. The successive scenes depicted how a spirit of fear was trying to bring destruction into people's lives with its lies, and the message each time was that fear is a liar. As the words to the song were displayed, there was the scene of a man who was attempting suicide because of a job termination. Another scene was of a young woman's emotional agony as she faced the bullying of her peers at school and the conflict with her mother that resulted. But one scene stood out from all the rest that played out before me, and my world stopped as I watched it.

A woman kissed her fingertips then lovingly touched a photograph on the wall of her home. The framed photo was of a dead son. Then moments later, in the video's next scene, she picked up a pamphlet from her coffee table with the title "Coping with Cancer." Short scenes followed showing the effects of the cancer treatments and its toll on her. There were the moments of crippling physical weakness from chemotherapy and her hair falling out onto her comb in front of her bathroom mirror, and in addition to it all, she was grieving for a lost son. There it was, the devastating grief over the death of a son, then a cancer diagnosis shortly after, and it was playing out in front of me in the video. It was my story. I broke down as I watched and sobbed openly at the table in front of my laptop where I sat. The song's music and its words surrounded me in those moments as I wept, and God's personal message for me was very clear. "Fear is a liar, Marguerite"

The previous day, a close friend had offered to pray for me at her prayer group's weekly meeting. That evening, I shared with her about God's message when He sang a song to me in the middle of the night and the video that I had viewed that morning. Her astonishment was evident as we spoke. She said, "Marguerite, that's the song we played specifically for you as we prayed for you last night!"

In the midst of life's storms, we must not be distracted by the light of the enemy's bonfires of lies. Those lies will erode our faith and consume us. They can shipwreck our faith in God. Jesus Christ is our lighthouse. In the midst of our trials and suffering, God will set us free from our fears if we allow Him to do so. Through my son's death and this cancer issue, the stronghold of fear in my life is coming down brick by brick, and I am overcoming the fear of dying and many other fears as well. When one has overcome fear, we are free to live, laugh, and love. Then we become free also to share the love of

God because there's no fear of losing anything anymore, and we have everything to gain. I have the promise of heaven and uninterrupted time with the living God in my future, as well as with all of my family who have gone before me. Whom or what do I have to fear?

I listened to the song and watched the video a second time the following morning. I didn't want to ever forget God's special message for me. He had sung a song to me in the night, asking me to trust Him, and that fear is a liar. When the video ended and as I reached over to shut off the music, the next song on the random playlist began. It was another Christian song, "You're Gonna Be OK" by Jenn Johnson. What? I'd never heard this song before. *Okay*, I thought, as I chuckled to myself. That just had to be coincidence, right? Five minutes later, I was in my car headed for work that day. As I turned my car on, the radio began to play. The first song that played? You guessed it, "Fear Is a Liar," and God threw down the mic.

Whose report will *you* believe?

Dear Randall,

How I miss you, son! All I have to do is think of you, and the tears come. At times, it's hard to speak of you in front of others. It's so easy to dissolve into the grief in the moment. You were my pride and joy, my handsome son, and so full of life. It was difficult living so far from you after I moved out of state. I wish you had moved with me. I desperately wanted you to. You had just turned eighteen, and the familiarity of friends and your grandparents prevailed, and you chose to stay behind. It tore me apart deeply to leave you that day.

This grief journey has been horrific. The pain as beyond description. In one brief moment, while looking at a photo of you recently, I also wanted to die. When your father passed at the age of thirty-two, his death was devastating for me. I'd never lost a loved one before. Now, you are also gone. It would be easy to wonder what I have done wrong to deserve these two death-dealing "blows" in my life.

A part of me wants to ask you why you did this to me. I feel robbed of a future with not only you but also of a future wife and grandchildren to come that you would have had. The thought of your having been in the grips of a drug addiction without me present to try to step in and help grieves me. Why did you hide this from me? I could have entered into the struggle of life with you to help you prevail somehow.

When you came to visit the last time and insisted that I pick you up at a motel the next day instead of the airport after your flight arrived, you were visibly shaking. I didn't understand why, and it disturbed me so deeply. I didn't know what to do, what to say. In hindsight, I realized that you chose to stay that night in the motel to

129

get past the drug withdrawal before you saw me. You were still going through it when I came to get you the next morning.

Did you know that I drive up to the same stoplight in front of the same motel every day that I go to see the oncologist for the radiation treatments? It's a block away from the cancer center. I feel sick inside when I see that motel every time. It stares me in the face at that stoplight. The memory of you standing there, shaking when I picked you up still haunts me. Oh, son, I feel so stupid and ignorant. Why didn't I see the signs of the addiction? I feel like I failed you. What could I have done to make a difference in your life so this would not prevail and take you from me? You were so loved and cherished by your father and myself. We planned for you and could not wait until you were born! Now, I can only hold on to the memories of your youth and all the wonderful things we did and shared as mother and son.

God went to great lengths to communicate to me that you are with Him, and for that, I am continuously and deeply grateful. But I still face, at times, the self-blame, the "would have," "could have," and "should haves" that come. Oh, Randall, do you have any idea what it was like facing the policeman on my doorstep that Sunday afternoon? You were my only child, my son, and he told me you were gone.

Always, all my love to you,
Mom

RUN THE RACE

I saw a jet-black stallion on a hill, finely muscled and sleek, in full rear on hind legs, pawing in the air in a majestic stance with the "look of eagles." This was a far cry from the starting gate where the stallion came from.

It had been bucking and thrashing against the confinement of a raceway's starting gate for some time. Wounds on the stallion's legs, flanks, and sides were already present from life's battering, and now the stallion's resistance to the gate's restrictions and confinement prevented any healing. The Master rider had been gently reaching over the rails of the gate to calm the stallion to bring it to a place of peace so that the wounds would heal first, and then it could run its race for Him.

The stallion learns to be still and to be healed. At the right moment then, the gate flashes open. The stallion charges out of the gate to run the race with steady force and purpose. There are no open wounds now or bruising to hinder its racing strength as it runs full tilt to the finish line. There is a calm, focused purpose in every great stride. The stallion is racing to win.

How many of us are stuck in the gate, wounded and thrashing? Are we allowing Christ to bring His healing to the woundedness of our hearts so we can run the race unfettered and finish well?

Do you not know that in a race all the runners run, but only one gets the prize? Run in such a way as to get the prize.

—1 Corinthians 9:24

GOD, THE THREE WITNESSES, AND...

As a Christian, by far, the greatest challenge I had to face when my son died was the uncertainty of where he stood with God. I heard him ask Christ into his heart and life as a child, but as a parent, you wonder if it was a child's simple imitation of the parent's conviction at the time or a true, heartfelt conversion. Did my son truly understand, as a child, what asking Jesus to come into his life meant? Many claim to know Christ but have no active relationship with Him.

My son was in the throes of addiction at the age of thirty-two. As he entered adulthood, it looked like he had abandoned his faith, and he seemed to live life as he pleased. As far as I knew, he was not really giving God a second thought. For a time, questions pummeled my mind relentlessly. Was he with God? I longed to know if he was with God and not lost to me forever and that I would see him again someday. True to His nature, God answered my heart's cry as only He could. He confirmed and reaffirmed in several different ways and through various circumstances over a two-year period of time that my son was with Him.

One of the biblical laws established by God in the Old Testament and also mentioned in the New was the law regarding witnesses. Two to three witnesses were required to confirm the truth or facts of a given situation, an event, or to determine the credibility of an accusation leveled against someone. The Scriptures state, "On the mouth of two to three witnesses a matter shall be confirmed" (Deuteronomy 19:15). And again, "This is the third time I am coming to you [Paul]. Every fact [word] is to be confirmed by the testimony [mouth] of two or three witnesses" (2 Corinthians 13:1).

133

We see this in our culture during court trials as witnesses are called forward to testify, to bear witness, or confirm the facts or truth about an event or person's actions. As Christians, we know that this is one avenue that God will use to speak to us when we need confirmation on an issue or an answer to an important question we've asked of God. Two or three people in succession, unrelated to each other, will confirm or communicate through what they say the same answer or direction God is giving. I have asked God for these confirmations on life issues and decisions many times over the years, so I know I am hearing Him accurately. God knew my deepest heart's question and my greatest fear that my son was not with Him. God wove into the week of my son's passing the testimony of the three witnesses for me.

As I stood in the flower shop, I was shocked at being handed a bill that was much less than expected for my son's funeral flowers. In fact, it was at cost, not retail. I began to see that God had arranged everything ahead of time. Every funeral arrangement being made fell into place seamlessly, as well as all financial needs were being met when I had none. I felt loved by God on a level I have never known before, and I was impacted and taken aback by the deep love God was exhibiting for my son through His timely and incredible provisions. A childlike amazement was embracing me in every moment as God's love and grace also carried me daily through that week. I called my pastor in Florida to tell him what God was doing. As I began to share with him what was happening, he interjected and said, "Marguerite, God is confirming that your son is with Him."

Pastor: Witness Number 1

The following day, the woman who had volunteered to sing for my son's funeral handed me what she said was my son's favorite hymn from the folder of music she carried. As she handed the sheet music to me, I was stunned and speechless. The first spiritual song I had learned as a child to play on my piano, which drew me to Christ decades beforehand, I was now holding the lyrics to that song in my hands. The funeral home's hospice pastor listened intently moments later as I shared with him this amazing "coincidence." He said, "Marguerite, God is confirming that your son is with Him."

Hospice Pastor: Witness Number 2

Randall's funeral was devastating for me, yet at the same time, it was an amazing living demonstration of the favor of God as He surrounded me daily with His love by His actions on my behalf. I also began to see with greater clarity that He loved my son even in the midst of his shortcomings, failures, and yes, the addictions. I thought to myself, *How could this be? Could it be that there was an inherent undercurrent in my belief system that has seen salvation as more about performance than God's love, and I had not recognized it?*

I began to realize through all of God's loving movements and confirmations that week that I am guilty—guilty of performance in my walk of faith more than I knew and that I was projecting it on to others too. My knowledge of the love of God was exposed as minuscule. My son gave me a gift in his death. That gift was the exposure of the underlying performance spiritually in my life. It was subtle and hidden. It's not about what I do or don't do or how well I do it, though disobedience can bring great hardship, harm, or destruction, and it did to my son. But it's about to whom I belong instead. This is about trusting that God's love will never fail. Through Randall's death, I was introduced to God's deep love for me that I never knew. Only God can know the heart of a man; we do not. And by the way, He can be trusted with that.

The evening I arrived home from Florida, I called the personnel coordinator at my place of employment to talk about returning to work at some point. I began to share about the movements of God that had transpired in the past week during my son's funeral. She startled me by abruptly interrupting what I was sharing in midsentence and said, "Marguerite, God is confirming that your son is with Him."

Coworker: Witness Number 3

Then eight months later, there was…

The Message for Me

It was my first Mother's Day without my son, my only child. No card, no phone call—it was heartbreaking. The holiday was on a Sunday this year. So needless to say, I grieved at church when they called the mothers forward for recognition and a gift. I grieved openly again at a friend's home during the holiday's midday dinner I was invited to. When I returned home that afternoon, there were numerous Facebook posts with messages of comfort from many friends, who knew of my grief on this first Mother's Day without my son. Every message meant so much yet brought even greater pain. One, however, stood out from all the rest, and it was from my nephew.

After my son's accidental overdose, I saw that God had begun to reach out to my nephew in the midst of his own addictions during the following weeks and months. When interacting with him during this time period in phone calls or in person, I noticed a distinct spiritual gifting from the Lord coming forward at times when he spoke. The call on his life and God's anointing, which I had known for some time was there, had surfaced intermittently even in the midst of his battle with addiction over the years.

The Mother's Day message he posted on Facebook was heartrending yet incredible. As I read it, I noticed a distinct change in the midst of his written message. There was a sentence in the message that seemed different and out of place, as though spoken by someone else (italicized in the post below). It grabbed my attention, and as I read it, I began to understand that God was allowing a message from my son to be sent to me, spoken by the Holy Spirit through my nephew. It was a message of promise and hope for the future. I broke down and wept uncontrollably as I read it and found out later that others were impacted by it as well.

Some will say that the Scriptures forbid contact with those who have passed, and that is true. However, in context, the Scriptures are referring to "consulting" the dead for guidance or direction specifically (i.e., séances, etc.). Time after time, I have heard testimonies of people over the years who have experienced a brief message in one form or another of reassurance from a loved one who had passed and is not guidance oriented.

I have had this happen with the passing of two other loved ones, my mother and my former husband. Interestingly enough, it did not occur after my dad's death, and I could not even begin to speculate as to why. I believe that at times, God lovingly allows a brief and final goodbye or sign that is meant to give hope for the eternal future in heaven ahead. The message was this:

> Today is a special day! Today is the day that we celebrate one of the best things God gave us, and that's mothers! I know that you may be having a hard time today, but there is one thing that I know and that's that Randall is soaring with angels and He (God) has left me here to remind you of that! *I love you with all my heart and soul MOM and just wanted you to remember that our time here is nothing compared to the time we will share later!* So let's thank Him for the little time and blessing we share now and enjoy this day He has given us here! (JT, Mother's Day, May 14, 2017)

Randall L. Woodall, 5/18/1984–10/2/2016

The Gentle Breeze

A s the woman sat down for a time of prayer, God's Spirit gently spoke to her with an image that came to mind. She saw a woman emerging from a bomb shelter. She had been hiding in it most of her life. Hiding there seemed to keep her from the continuous bombardments of life, the strafing, the assaults of the enemy as a child and adult through family, friends, and circumstances in life's journey.

As she stepped out into the light of life, she began to see the mountains, lakes, and all the scenic beauty around her. It was wonderful to breathe in fresh air, and her favorite moment was a gentle breeze blowing through her hair—you know, the same breeze that passed by Elijah long ago.

> (9) Then he came there to a cave and spent the night there; and behold, the word of the Lord came to him, and He said to him, "What are you doing here, Elijah?" (10) And he said, "I have been very zealous for the Lord, the God of armies; for the sons of Israel have abandoned Your covenant, torn down Your altars, and killed Your prophets with the sword. And I alone am left; and they have sought to take my life."
>
> (11) So He said, "Go out and stand on the mountain before the Lord." And behold, the Lord was passing by! And a great and powerful wind was tearing out the mountains and breaking the rocks in pieces before the Lord; but the Lord was not in the wind. And after the wind

there was an earthquake, but the Lord was not in the earthquake. (12) And after the earthquake, a fire, but the Lord was not in the fire; and after the fire, a sound of a gentle blowing. 13) When Elijah heard it, he wrapped his face in his cloak and went out and stood in the entrance of the cave. (1 Kings 19:9–13 NASB)

I saw an ancient city down below as we stood side by
side on a hill nearby. The sun seemed to be setting for
the evening, and a glowing sunset was in the sky above
it. I turned to Him and asked Him a question.

Q: "Lord, do you know how hard it is to keep going
forward despite what I feel or how bad I hurt?"
A: Placing His hand on my arm, as we
stood there, He said, "I know."

And He resolutely set His face to go toward Jerusalem.

—Luke 9:51

The greater the conflicts and struggles are, the deeper the well of character can be dug. Deep wells do not run dry and can be counted on to slack the thirst of those seeking the Truth.

—Marguerite Lever Woodall

THE SCROLL OF DESTINY

We all have a book or scroll of destiny. Written down in
these scrolls are the works God has predestined for every
one of us to walk in in our life journey. It is not destiny
as the world views it, and we can refuse to live it.

This scroll is sealed. When opened, the greater works God has
planned for us to do to glorify Him begin. Only Jesus can break open
the seal. His sacrifice is what qualified Him to do so for every man.

Please remember that all men have a scroll with God's specific
works for them written out in it. It is held for them when they
first receive salvation and is opened only in God's time.

When God sees that we have come to a place in our life where we
can be trusted with these works that were laid out for us by Him,
Christ will open the scroll, and it is time for these events to begin.

Sadly, very few people have submitted enough in
their life to God so that Christ can open it.

For we are His workmanship, created in Christ
Jesus for good works, which God prepared
beforehand, that we should walk in them.

—Ephesians 2:10

THE VALUED

The feelings of aloneness can be overwhelming when you've lost everyone or someone of great importance in your life. Lostness—it walks with you for a time when you grieve. As I drove home yesterday, I recognized the source of another area of pain in my life I couldn't quite put my finger on for some time during the grieving process. Your children value you as their mother if not estranged from you. The loss of my only child has ripped away my valuation as a mother. It is gone. Did I forget to mention the love and value given by possible future grandchildren as their grandmother? This has been taken too (what's known as a secondary loss). What do you do with that? I don't know what to do with that.

There was a moment when God stepped in and brought some revelation that I needed badly. The tears began streaming down my face as I drove my car home one particular night as it hit me. It was the realization that the death of my husband so many years before had stripped away a relationship with someone who valued me deeply. Part of my deepest desire in life is to have a companion again, a husband. Now I understand that part of this desire is because of a lack of feeling valued as a woman because of my former husband's absence. As a side thought, how many of us have married the wrong person for this reason?

I face losing what physical attraction I thought I had as I struggle with the effects of medications prescribed after the cancer surgery and the radiation sessions. There's the loss of some of my hair, and by the way, where did my eyebrows go? The hip and joint pain as I sleep, at times, has been overwhelming. The symptoms of arthritis are being exacerbated daily by the cancer drug. A titanic struggle to keep myself from gaining weight has ensued because of it. I had not expected nor did I think about possible side effects from the cancer treatments.

Do I sound petty? Yes. This is the truth, and I know it's ugly. But then Jesus specializes and deals with "ugly," and I'm so glad. Any value I've placed on myself in my appearance and being attractive is vanishing bit by bit. I struggle with this every day. The death of a misplaced value on ourselves dies hard.

Yes, I've heard all the trite answers or responses from those who mean well—you know, the comments about finding your value in Christ and such. Know your value from God's perspective. But how does that work itself out? What does that look like? Just how does God relate to us in a way in the present and our daily living that answers and dispels or dismantles all the illegitimate value systems in our lives that we've adopted or that life teaches us? There's certainly nothing wrong with being cherished by a husband, but I'm slowly realizing that it must come from God first.

This is a part of the journey with Christ, and I believe few have walked it. The "stripping down" of some aspect of our flesh, physical or otherwise, that has dictated our value or worth apart from God's. Not many choose to let God bring this about. Those who have found that path and understood it come out the other side as some of the most grace-filled, powerful people you can meet. I know one, and when she speaks of walking through the death of the misplaced physical value of herself that God brought about, it is with a rapture that has discovered the deep valuation placed on her by God instead. I want that. The love of God emanates from her like a gentle-yet-powerful light. I am grateful (believe it or not) that God is showing me how I have falsely valued myself for so long, a lifetime. How it will work itself out, I do not know, but I'm headed in that direction with the Lord leading me moment by moment and challenge by challenge.

Just a few years ago, I saw a woman walking toward a great light. She was dressed in a lovely, brilliant white gown that shimmered and was much like a ball gown. Her face was tilted upward in expectation, looking forward as she walked with her gaze focused on the Father. The look of "I am loved" on her face was beyond human words to describe as I gazed at her. The love so animated her face that her countenance emanated a great light, the light of God. That light was meant to glorify Him in every way because of His love.

When I saw her image in my spirit I thought, *This is the face of someone who knows how deeply they are loved by God, and it shines a great light everywhere!* I called this image "the face of light and loved." It was me. He dared to show me where He wants to take me as I walk with him in the arena of His valuation. It was one of those moments when He showed me an image of the future He has planned for my life. I now have a promise of what I am going to become in my journey with Him.

SAFELY HOME

It's almost four years now since my son passed. Yesterday would have been his thirty-sixth birthday. The entire month of May has been full of challenges over the years. My husband was killed May 8, my mother died Mother's Day weekend, my son's birthday was on May 18, and the actual holiday of Mother's Day has become painful now too. For some reason, at the three-year mark of my son's passing, I struggled terribly. I pondered why the three-year mark hit me so hard. One would think that the opposite would be true. The greater passage of time, the grief would lessen, right?

It was the amount of the time that had passed without the inter-action of my loved one that brought home the full reality of the absence of my son. Time's distance drove the event home. He really is gone. Before the three-year anniversary, I had still found myself say-ing off and on, "I can't believe this really happened." Now, this fourth year is different. It was still painful of course, and the grief showed up as usual, but I am healing, and I walked through this month much more at peace than ever before. At times, I'm rather blown away by how long the journey for me has been to just accept the reality of what has happened.

When I've shared about how the month of May has such a hard history in my life, a godly woman I know popped up and said, "Let's pray that God redeems the month of May for you!" What an awe-some thought! And so I have prayed and others have also for God to redeem this particular month for me. I've wondered at times what that redemption will look like.

In my time of prayer this particular morning, I had some real random thoughts as I conversed and shared my heart with God. I had two questions for Him, and I thought later that God would probably consider them unimportant. My first question was this: did Jesus meet my son at heaven's entrance, or did he see Christ later (as some have testified in near-death experiences) after being in heaven for a time?

The second question was related to the cancer issue I had recently been through shortly after my son died. There are very few of us who've had cancer who do not go through the constant nagging thought that the cancer will return and return with a vengeance. We live with this "backdrop" in our thoughts every day. The adversary (Satan) has a way of trying to tear a person down with fearful thoughts about this. It's much like a Damocles Sword hanging over them.

I then asked Him my second question: would my life be cut short for one reason or another before I can finish what God has called me to do? Like anyone else who is a follower of Christ, the time I am given matters in what I'm hoping the Lord will achieve through me. After asking God these two questions, I then dismissed them as unimportant in the overall scheme of things, and I certainly did not expect an answer. After all, did that really matter?

There was another day of work ahead for me, and as I arrived that same morning, my coworker and friend Kay approached me immediately with an envelope in hand. As she gave it to me, she said, "Marguerite, the Lord told me to write this and give it to you." Slipped inside the purple-colored envelope was a poem, carefully handwritten, that was titled "Safely Home." On the notepaper were the answers to the two questions (in italics) I had so offhandedly asked God that morning about my son and my life. I cried unabashedly standing there on that grocery store aisle, marveling at how my loving Father reached out to me to answer both questions so quickly and ahead of time, when really I had expected none.

SAFELY HOME

I am now at home in heaven;
All's so happy, all so bright!
There as perfect joy and beauty
In this everlasting light.

All the pain and grief are over,
Every restless tossing past;
I am now at peace forever,
Safely home in heaven at last.

Did you wonder I so calmly
trod the Valley of the Shade?
Oh! But Jesus love illuminated
Every dark and fearful glade.

And He came Himself to meet me
In that way so hard to tread;
And with Jesus arm to lean on,
Could I have one doubt or dread?

Then you must not grieve so sorely,
For I love you dearly still;
Try to look beyond earth's shadows,
Pray to trust our Father's will.

There is work still waiting for you,
So you must not idle stand;
Do your work while life remaineth—
You shall rest in Jesus land.

When that work is all completed,
He will gently call you home;
Oh, the rapture of the meeting!
Oh, the joy to see you come!

(Author Anonymous)

This answer from God occurred on May 20, two days after my son's birthday this year. The redemption of the month of May has begun.

THE MESSAGE

*To the one who let Me and is letting Me bring
My transformation and change; to the one who
has and is letting Me shape them through their pain...*

*And I say also to the one who fails or falters,
yet gets up and keeps following Me...*

You are one of My greatest redemption stories!

ABOUT THE AUTHOR

M rs. Woodall is a native of Eastern Oregon, was a longtime resident of Florida, and currently resides in Oklahoma as a florist by profession. Widowed at the age of thirty-two with a small child, experiencing her only child's death and a cancer diagnosis a year and a half later deepened the foundation of a developing intimacy in knowing God that has brought her through an unusual life journey.

After carrying a draw from within by God for many years that she would be writing a book at some point in her lifetime; this time has come. With a passion to tell the stories of God's interactions in her life and what is possible for others, it has become a mandate and purpose that has compelled Marguerite to this point and this book. In a moment of God's speaking clearly to her as her mother passed away, he shared that despite the tragedies and hardships here in this life, there are good things yet to come.